Hockey's Great Rivalries

Exciting accounts of the great individual and team duels in recent hockey history.

30
NORTHLAND
B
VICTORIAVILLE

Hockey's Great Rivalries

by Stan Fischler

illustrated with photographs

Random House
New York

This book is dedicated to hockey fans young and old, but especially to some of the most delightful, passionate and insightful rooters I have ever met—Paul Gardella, Ira Gitler, Mike Cosby, Bob Stampleman, Mickey Hopp, Mike Rubin and Howard Hyman.

PHOTOGRAPH CREDITS: Denis Brodeur, 142–43; Camera 5, 104; Camera 5—Ken Regan, 98; Canada Wide from Pictorial Parade, 9, 13, 26, 90–91, 128–129; Bernie Moser—Dufor Photographers, 122; Pictorial Parade, 85; Tass from Sovfoto, endpapers, 136–137, 139, 144; United Press International, 2–3, 21, 31, 36, 39, 43, 45, 50, 55, 60, 64, 71, 74, 76, 81, 109, 119, 131, 146; Wide World Photos, 18, 95, 101, 111, 114.
COVER: Photo by Dan Baliotti—Movement Associates

Library of Congress Cataloging in Publication Data
Fischler, Stan. Hockey's great rivalries. (Pro hockey library)
SUMMARY: Describes the rivalries between some of hockey's greatest individuals and teams: Bobby Orr vs. Brad Park, the Chicago Black Hawks vs. the Montreal Canadiens, and others.
1. Hockey—History—Juvenile literature. (1. Hockey) I. Title.
GV846.5.F56 1974 796.9'62 74-4930
ISBN 0-394-82830-5 ISBN 0-394-92830-X (lib. Bdg.)

Manufactured in the United States of America 1 2 3 4 5 6 7 8 9 0

Contents

Introduction

As a hockey nut growing up in Brooklyn in the early 1940s, I viewed the rivalry between the Toronto Maple Leafs and the Detroit Red Wings as the ultimate hockey battle.

It was, too. But in the years since, many other classic confrontations have come and gone, and every season brings more. Whether the contestants are two individuals like Bobby Orr and Brad Park or two great teams, their head-to-head meetings are what make the game go.

Hockey rivalries erupt as regularly as the dropping of a puck. On these pages I have tried to present a few of the sport's major confrontations. Hopefully I have touched on one of the reader's favorites, but in any case I have tried to convey some of the excitement and fury that have made hockey the fastest-growing international sport.

STAN FISCHLER

Hockey's Great Rivalries

Montreal Canadiens vs. Chicago Black Hawks

No two teams in the National Hockey League clubs seemed more different than the proud Montreal Canadiens and the rough-and-tumble Chicago Black Hawks. Over many seasons, the Canadiens had developed a "mystique," an indefinable will and ability to win hockey games—and Stanley Cups. By contrast, Chicago always seemed to live up to its title as the Second City—second to New York in most things, but second to Montreal in hockey.

The Stanley Cup records proved Chicago's hockey standing. Through 1970, Montreal had won hockey's world championship a record 15 times while Chicago had won only twice. Yet in the 1960s and early 1970s the Black Hawks became the envy of their Montreal foe. They did so by producing a galaxy of spectacular stars such as Bobby Hull, Stan Mikita, Tony Esposito and Pat Stapleton. The team won the Cup only once in the 1960s, but Hull's angels attracted huge crowds wherever they played.

The Canadiens accented both offense and defense. But the Black Hawks were concerned with scoring goals and more goals. Mikita, the clever center, ladled pinpoint passes to the wings and Bobby Hull perfected the hardest slapshot ever seen on ice. "When Bobby shoots," said Pittsburgh goalie Les Binkley, "the puck moves so fast it looks like a little pea."

The first contest in what became a fierce rivalry between Montreal and Chicago came in the spring of 1965 when the Canadiens and Black Hawks met head-on in the Stanley Cup finals. Coached by Billy Reay, the Black Hawks had finished third, while the Montrealers, under the direction of Toe Blake, finished second with seven more points in the standings.

To reach the finals, Montreal had defeated Toronto while Chicago edged Detroit. Then the proud Montrealers and the determined Chicagoans battled through six games, each club winning three. On May 1, 1965, they met on Montreal's Forum ice in the decisive seventh game. Within 14 seconds captain Jean Beliveau of the Canadiens had scored against Black Hawk goalie Glenn Hall. The Canadiens added three more tallies, winning the game 4–0 and carrying off the Stanley Cup.

The Flying Frenchmen from Montreal met the Black Hawks once again in the 1968 semifinals, and whipped them four games to one en route to still another world championship.

It wasn't until April 1970 that the Hawks exacted some revenge, and in a most curious way. Chicago was

Black Hawk Bobby Hull (right) and Canadien Jean Beliveau, two hockey superstars, chase the puck in a 1968 game.

first in the NHL's East Division going into the final night of the season, but Montreal was battling tooth-and-nail with New York for the fourth place—and a chance to play in the Stanley Cup series.

The Rangers had played their last game of the season on the afternoon of April 5, defeating Detroit at Madison Square Garden. Montreal was scheduled to face Chicago that evening at Chicago Stadium. In order to beat out the Rangers, the Canadiens had to win or tie the Black Hawks. If they lost, they would end up in a tie with New York. Then fourth place would be decided by which team had the most goals for the season. On the evening of April 5, the Rangers were four goals ahead. So Montreal had one other slim chance to make the playoffs—they could actually lose to Chicago *if* they scored five goals.

All that remained in the Canadiens' way were the Black Hawks with their high-scoring forwards and goalie Tony Esposito. After Montreal got an early goal from Yvan Cournoyer, the Black Hawks stormed to the attack and in no time at all Jim Pappin, Pit Martin and Bobby Hull had given the Chicago sextet a 3–1 lead. Jean Beliveau scored a second time for Montreal, but early in the third period, Black Hawk Martin busted the game wide open with two more scores. With 10:44 remaining, the Hawks led 5–2.

It was then that Canadiens coach Claude Ruel tried a bizarre tactic to qualify for the playoffs. He ordered goalie Rogatien Vachon off the ice and inserted an extra forward in his place. Ruel was conceding the victory to the Black Hawks, but hoped the extra forward would help score three more goals.

"What could I do?" said Ruel afterward. "We needed goals if we were to make the playoffs."

A less-determined team than the Black Hawks might have wilted under Montreal's pressure but the Chicago skaters had something to prove and they socked to the Canadiens at every turn until the final buzzer. The scoreboard said it all—Chicago 10, Montreal 2!

So the Black Hawks had their revenge, and if the Canadiens were bitter about anyone it was goalie Esposito, who had flip-flopped all over the ice in a desperate effort to thwart every Montreal drive. Esposito had once been a member of the Montreal organization and had been dropped because they didn't think he was good enough for the NHL, so he had good reason to be happy with his performance against six attackers.

Ironically, it was Tony's brother Phil Esposito who spoiled the fun for Tony that spring. In the semifinals, Phil's Bruins blasted the Black Hawks four games to none and Phil was the high-scorer.

Once again the Black Hawks had come up empty at the Stanley Cup well. They ached for another chance at the silverware and they got it the next season in a severe hand-to-hand struggle for the Cup. What had been a simmering rivalry between the Black Hawks and the Canadiens exploded into a flaming hatred by the time they were through with each other. The two teams met in the finals of the Stanley Cup after bruising encounters in the earlier rounds. The Canadiens had suffered at the hands of the tough, physical Boston Bruins in the opening round. The Bruins had the best regular season record in the league and were heavily favored, but Montreal had reached an emotional high and won in seven games. With the upset behind them, the Frenchmen suffered a natural letdown and had unexpected difficulties in beating the Minnesota North Stars in the semifinals. Some experts thought Montreal had lost its competitive edge.

By contrast, the Black Hawks seemed to be entering the series at their competitive peak. Chicago had swept Philadelphia in the first round with an ease that was almost embarrassing. Hull and company rode in on the Flyers' goal all but unchallenged. And at the other end of the ice Tony Esposito was seldom put to a severe test. But in the second round, against the Rangers, it was an entirely different story. In one of the best series in Stanley Cup history, the Hawks eliminated New York in seven games, three of them decided in overtime periods. In the seventh and deciding game Chicago had rallied from a 2–1 deficit midway in the second period to win by a score of 4–2. The Hawks were exhausted after the Ranger series but they were still mentally and competitively up for the finals. That was one reason the majority of experts picked Chicago to win the Stanley Cup.

Against the Rangers, the Hawks' Tony Esposito had outplayed the league's All-Star goalie, Ed Giacomin, and there was little reason to believe Esposito would be any less effective against the Canadiens. By contrast, Montreal goalie Ken Dryden had played only six NHL games before the playoff began. He had been spectacular against Boston, but he had been less than that against the North Stars. And there was some doubt that he could withstand the pressure of a Stanley Cup final with so little experience.

Then, too, Chicago's defensive tandem of Bill White and Pat Stapleton had shown in the New York series that they ranked with the best, improving Chicago's traditional weak spot. And finally, there was Bobby Hull. He had scored two winning goals against the Rangers—one in overtime and the one in the seventh game. The Rangers had come close to neutralizing Hull by assigning a "shadow" to follow him wherever he went, but his only two goals were winners. Montreal had its own shadow ready—twenty-one-year-old Rejean Houle—but could a relatively inexperienced youngster like Houle handle the likes of Bobby Hull?

The series opened in Chicago on May 4. Outside Chicago Stadium it was hot and humid. Inside, 20,000 fans took up every available seat and just about every inch of standing room. They roared a raucous welcome as the Black Hawks skated onto the ice. For the Canadiens there was a chorus of boos, a tradition with rabid Chicago fans.

There was no scoring in the first period. Each team seemed to be feeling out the other. Both appeared sharp. "I was worried about the game for about the first couple of minutes," Chicago coach Billy Reay said later, "and then I knew we were ready."

The Hawks did have the better of play in the first period. Dryden was called on to make some tough saves. The second period, however, was different. The Frenchmen came out flying and the Hawks quickly became disorganized. As Montreal continued to put pressure on Esposito, it seemed only a matter of time until they would break through. Finally they did, on a picture-play goal by Jacques Lemaire. And the Canadiens were playing so well they seemed able to hold

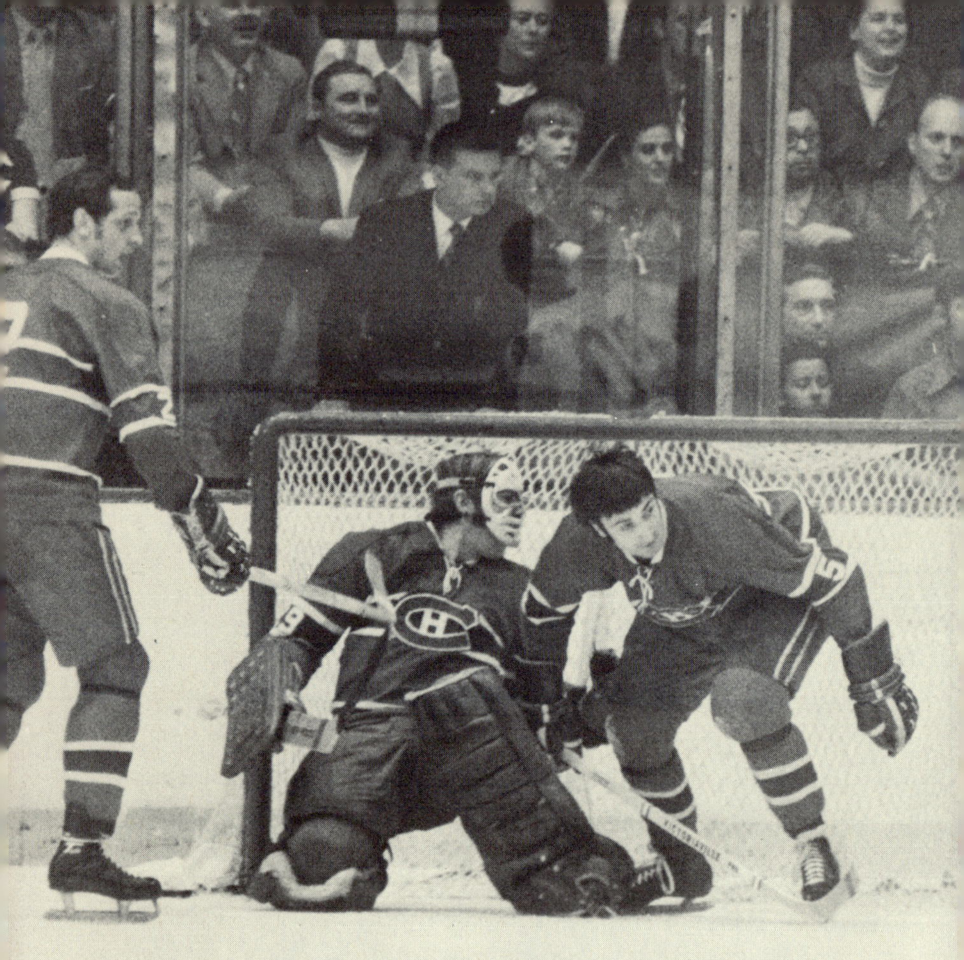

Canadien goalie Ken Dryden gets some unexpected help from defenseman Guy LaPointe in the 1971 Stanley Cup playoffs against Chicago.

Chicago scoreless and net a few more goals.

But in the third period the game turned around again. Suddenly the Hawks were pressing. Dryden made some spectacular saves, but now there was that feeling that Chicago would break through before the game was over. Just before the midway point of the period, Bobby Hull scored and the game was tied.

It stayed that way through the rest of the third period. Jim Pappin had a chance to win the game for the Hawks late in the session, but Dryden made another great save. Early in the first overtime period, Frank Mahovlich came close for the Canadiens, but Esposito stopped *him*. But Chicago seemed to be growing stronger while the Canadiens seemed to grow less certain and more tired as the game wore on.

Then, one minute into the second overtime period, Pappin carried the puck across the Montreal blue line. Canadiens Yvan Cournoyer and Terry Harper leveled him with a vicious bodycheck and the puck skidded free to the right side of the Montreal net. Stan Mikita got to it first. Two Canadiens converged on Mikita as Pappin scrambled to his feet. Mikita moved in on Dryden.

"I gave Dryden every fake I knew," Mikita said later. Then, when he was only seven or eight feet in front of the net, he passed to Pappin and Pappin slammed the puck into the net.

"I didn't see Pappin at all," Dryden said later. "As soon as Mikita passed it, I sprawled, but it was much too late."

For the young goaltender it was an especially heartbreaking defeat. He had stopped 56 Chicago shots. In the Montreal dressing room there was a sense of gloom.

"The goalies certainly dominated this game," said

Montreal coach Al MacNeil to reporters. "There were some great saves out there. But overtime is one big play; a mistake by one side and it's all over." Then, referring to Chicago's overall home-ice advantage, MacNeil added, "We've got to get one game here."

For a time it looked as though the Canadiens would "get one game" in the second match. The Hawks had scored first, Bobby Hull putting the puck past Dryden during a power play. But the Canadiens bounced back with two before the first period was over on a power-play goal by Lemaire and a score by Peter Mahovlich. Mahovlich's goal was especially pretty, as he "deked" Esposito to the ice and then put the puck behind him with a sharp backhand shot. The Canadiens continued to dominate the play early in the second period and might have gone on to win had it not been for Chicago's favorite "utility" player, Lou Angotti.

His first contribution went unnoticed by many. Early in the second period Chicago's Chico Maki let fly with a long shot from just inside the Montreal blue line. Dryden barely moved as the puck flew past him and into the net—his view of the shot was blocked by Lou Angotti.

"I wouldn't have had the goal if it wasn't for Lou," Maki said after the game. "He set up the perfect screen for me."

With that quick, unexpected goal, the momentum shifted to the Black Hawks. Less than two minutes after Maki's goal, Pappin scored. So at the end of two periods Chicago led, 3–2.

Early in the third period it was still anyone's game.

Chicago's Jim Pappin (left) is about to score, putting the Black Hawks ahead in the second playoff game.

Then, a clearing pass by Montreal's J. C. Tremblay bounced off the boards and onto Angotti's stick. Lou shot and the Hawks were two goals up, 4–2. Frank Mahovlich cut the margin to 1 with his twelfth score of the playoffs, only to have Angotti put the game out of reach by stealing the puck from Tremblay in the Montreal zone and scoring again. Black Hawks 5, Montreal 3.

"When I got control of the puck I thought I was too close to Dryden," Angotti said in describing his second goal. "Dryden came out and when I made a move to the right, he didn't move. So I shot. Usually I fall on my face on plays like that."

In the Montreal dressing room Tremblay was philosophical about his errors. "I've made mistakes before," he said. "I don't brood over them. I have no excuses. He just made a good play. You could say I made a star out of Angotti."

"We were overcautious in the overtime of the first game," MacNeil said. "We started the second game well, taking it to them and controlling play, but we seemed to go flat and the Hawks took it away from us.

"You need 60 minutes together in this game," MacNeil added. "You've got to work extra hard against a team like this. You can't make mistakes."

But the next two games would be played in Montreal, and Chicago's coach, Billy Reay, was cautious: "Don't kid yourself. Those Montrealers aren't out of this yet."

For the first period of the third game the Canadiens

were flat, the Black Hawks confident. Montreal had shots on goal, but could not mount a sustained attack. The Canadiens' defensemen were hesitant. Even Dryden looked somewhat uncertain.

At 3:09 of the first period Peter Mahovlich was sent to the penalty box for elbowing, and the Hawks quickly capitalized on their one-man advantage. Mikita started the scoring play by taking the puck from defenseman Guy Lapointe along the right boards deep in Montreal ice. He sent the puck to Bobby Hull on the right point. Hull faked a slapshot, then slid the puck to Cliff Koroll, who was skating right-to-left past the Montreal goal. Koroll fired from fifteen feet out and Dryden didn't have a chance.

Ten minutes later the Hawks scored again. Pit Martin passed from the right point to Pappin, who was stationed to the left of the Montreal goal. Pappin backhanded the puck to the goalmouth and Bobby Hull jammed it home. Even though Chicago was outshot in the first period, 13–8, it looked as if the Hawks were in complete control of the game with a 2–0 lead. But it only looked that way.

"It's kind of tough to outshoot them in the first period and come up empty," Peter Mahovlich said later. "But we decided we wouldn't stay empty and we didn't." Al MacNeil talked to his players between periods and told them, "Keep skating and keep driving, because we're outshooting them and something has to happen."

Montreal's Peter Mahovlich made something happen

at 5:56 of the second period. He took the puck away from Black Hawk Keith Magnuson in the right corner of the Chicago zone, wheeled, took three big strides back toward the blue line, then snapped the puck past Tony Esposito from twenty feet out. Now it was 2–1.

Within minutes it became obvious that the tide had turned. Chicago faltered and was penalized. The Canadiens swarmed in on Esposito. But Tony would not let the puck go in, and the home fans began to think that perhaps the Canadiens weren't destined to win this one. At 13:44 the Hawks' Jim Pappin was hit with a double penalty that would keep him off the ice for four minutes. Despite the one-man advantage the Canadiens could not score. During that stretch Chicago defensemen Stapleton (who was playing with fifty stitches in his face from being cut by a skate) and White were tremendous.

Then, at 16:03 Bobby Hull was penalized. For the next minute-and-a-half Montreal had a two-man advantage. The Canadiens applied tremendous pressure. But with Mikita, White and Stapleton in front of him, Esposito held firm. At one point the Canadiens actually skated carousel-fashion in front of Tony, unloading a series of shots. Every one was blocked. Peter Mahovlich, watching in disbelief on the Montreal bench, slammed his stick against the ice.

Finally, just ten seconds before Pappin was due back on the ice, Frank Mahovlich circled to a spot directly in front of the Chicago net and 55 feet out. He fired the puck through a screen of players and past Esposito.

His goal tied the game at 2-all. Had the Hawks hung on for another ten seconds, the course of the whole series might have been different. In such moments are Stanley Cups won and lost.

At the start of the third period the 17,441 fans jammed into Montreal's Forum that Sunday afternoon began to cheer. The Canadiens were controlling play and their every move met with approval—with one exception. Defenseman Terry Harper, who had been victimized on Bobby Hull's goal in the first period, was still being booed.

"At first I wasn't aware of the crowd being on me," Harper said later, "but you know, I guess it does bother my playing."

In this instance, however, the jeers and catcalls lit a fire under him. Six-and-a-half minutes into the third period he started a rush from his own zone. He carried the puck across mid-ice and into the Chicago end, got by Keith Magnuson and shot the puck around the boards from the right-hand side to the left corner.

"I picked it up there again," Harper said, "and then Stan Mikita tried to hit me, but I got away from him. Then Magnuson had another try, and I bumped him and then went back for the puck. I looked out in front and saw both Cournoyer and Ferguson all alone and I couldn't believe it."

Harper passed the puck to Cournoyer and he shot it by the helpless Esposito. The crowd went wild. This time the cheers were for Harper. The game was Montreal's. Frank Mahovlich scored again at 12:13 to

Brothers Frank and Pete Mahovlich were Canadien heroes in the third and fourth games of the series.

make the score 4–2, but that was just icing on the cake. In that final period Chicago managed just four shots on goal and in the last minutes the Chicago defense broke down completely. Only some superlative goaltending by Esposito kept the score respectable. The Canadiens were back in the Stanley Cup series.

Certainly the fourth game was the most one-sided of the series. Peter Mahovlich scored first for Montreal, tipping in Terry Harper's point shot at the one-minute mark. Mikita tied it for Chicago two minutes later on a power play. Three minutes later Beliveau put the Canadiens ahead to stay and a goal by Guy Lapointe ten minutes after that made it a 3–1 game at the end of the first period.

Nine minutes into the second period, Chicago rookie Rick Foley tried to shoot the puck across his own blue line. Instead, he put it onto the stick of Montreal's Cournoyer, who had just stepped out of the penalty box. The speedy Montrealer cruised in and scored on Esposito and it was 4–1. Both teams scored once more, but the game had been decided. The scoreless third period was notable only for a few skirmishes and for the Montreal crowd's singing of "*Les Canadiens Sont La*" (The Canadiens Are Here), the team's traditional fight song. The most significant fact of the game was that Chicago's Bobby Hull had been limited to only two shots on goal by his young shadow, Rejean Houle.

Most hockey observers now agreed that the Canadiens would win the Cup. They had momentum and confidence. Goalie Dryden had played extremely well, and Montreal's offense and defense had meshed in games three and four. Chicago, on the other hand, and particularly its defense, looked tired and sluggish. Doug Jarrett and Keith Magnuson had been especially disappointing and there were reports, angrily denied by coach Reay, that Esposito was playing with an assortment of injuries.

Back in Chicago for the fifth game, the Black Hawks promptly proved that hockey predictions are hazardous, especially in Stanley Cup play. Chicago turned around and defeated Montreal, 2–0, largely on the play of Magnuson, Jarrett and Esposito, with a little inspirational help from Bobby Hull, who started hitting Canadiens early and often.

Esposito had 31 saves. Jarrett, meanwhile, was hitting people, handling the puck effectively in his own zone and moving it well on offense. Chicago got its first goal midway in the first period when Dennis Hull converted a goal-mouth pass from Cliff Koroll and a second, by Koroll, in the second period.

"The Hulls did all the work on the first goal," Koroll said later. "Bobby fed me the puck at the blue line. I went deep around Laperriere and passed out into the slot. Dennis had to muscle two Canadiens out of the way to reach the pass and score. His was the major effort."

Over in the Montreal dressing room Al MacNeil wasn't saying much, but Henri Richard was. "He's the worst coach I ever played for in my whole career," Henri told newsmen. He complained about MacNeil's juggling of lines and players during the fifth game, and was particularly bitter that he had been given little ice time after the first period.

"I always gave 100 per cent, I never loafed and I didn't deserve to be benched," Richard continued. "I'm paid to play. We had three sets of lines when we won [the fourth game]. What gives him the right to change it all? It's about time someone said what everyone on the team is thinking. How can you expect us to win like that?"

Richard rubbed salt in the wound by suggesting that MacNeil was a minor-league coach. "It may be easy to win games by frequent line changes with a club like the Voyageurs [a Montreal farm team], but it doesn't work like that in the National Hockey League."

MacNeil replied that no player had complained when the team was winning. "In this business you get used to these things from players who are unhappy at being benched or not getting enough ice time," he said.

The next day Richard said he should have kept his mouth shut, but he didn't take back his statement. Everyone on the team tried to play down the argument between the coach and the team's most venerable star. They could only hope that Richard could light a fire under the team—they needed two straight games if they were to regain the Stanley Cup.

The sixth game, at Montreal, was a Stanley Cup classic. It began with the first penalty shot in Stanley Cup history. "The Big M," Frank Mahovlich, was chasing a loose puck deep in the Chicago zone with no one but Esposito to beat. Esposito came out of his net, trying to beat Mahovlich to the puck. When he saw he would lose the race and leave an empty net for Mahovlich to shoot at, Esposito threw his stick at the puck and referee Art Skov immediately signaled for the historic penalty shot.

And so, in the sudden stillness of the Forum, at 4:43 of the first period one of hockey's most feared shooters went one-on-one against one of hockey's finest goalies.

Esposito won the duel.

"Esposito came out earlier than I expected, and then he started to get back, and I shot too early," Frank said later. "It hit his stick. It was a good shot, but it could have been higher. It would have been better if I had 'moved' him first. I should have gone in slower and made him move first."

From that point on Chicago forced the play. Jim Pappin scored at 11:25 of the first period to give the Hawks the lead. In a brilliant individual effort, Pappin skated around Lemaire and Lapointe and beat Dryden from close-in. But scarcely more than a minute later Cournoyer tied the game, assisted by Frank Mahovlich and Beliveau.

At the start of the second period Montreal took control. Three minutes into the period Lemaire capped a Montreal rush with a shot into the net. But the goal was disallowed because Chicago defenseman Pat Stapleton had knocked the net from its moorings—intentionally or otherwise. It was a disappointment for the

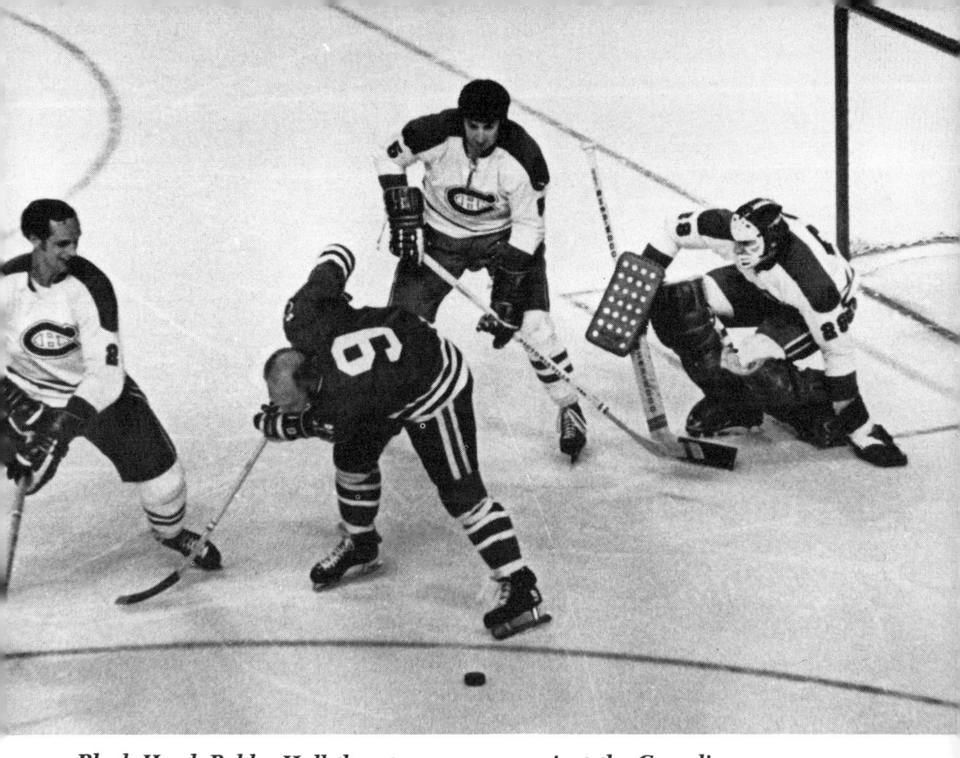

Black Hawk Bobby Hull threatens a score against the Canadiens.

Canadiens, but they didn't slow down. At 5:04, Peter Mahovlich put Montreal ahead, 2–1.

Then Chicago began pressing and soon regained the edge in play. In all, the Hawks had fourteen shots on goal that second period to Montreal's six, and two of Chicago's shots beat Dryden. The first was by Chico Maki at 17:40 and the second by Pappin at 18:38, on another outstanding solo effort. Skating right to left inside the Montreal zone, he went around Terry Harper, faked Laperriere and beat Dryden with a backhander. Chicago led 3–2, and the Canadiens were twenty minutes from elimination.

The first five minutes of the third period were fairly even. Then, after a Chicago "icing," Angotti and Beliveau faced off in the Chicago zone. The puck rolled free and out toward the blue line. Black Hawk Bill White put down his stick to capture it.

"The puck bounced on me," he said later. "I couldn't get my stick on it."

Frank Mahovlich got the puck, went around White and shot. Esposito blocked it, but the puck rolled free. Chicago's Stapleton went for it, but "The Big M" got there first and shot again—this time into the empty corner of the net. The goal was Frank's fourteenth of the playoffs, a Stanley Cup record. More important, the Canadiens were tied at 3–3.

At 8:04, Rejean Houle was penalized for holding Bobby Hull and Chicago had a golden opportunity to regain the lead. At 8:50, in a face-off on Chicago ice just inside the blue line, Lou Angotti failed to get a clean draw and the puck bounced free. Chicago players became entangled with one another. Frank Mahovlich got the puck first and passed it to his brother Peter, who was breaking in on the Chicago goal all alone. He shot and the puck caught the net. The Forum exploded in cheers as the Canadiens took the lead, 4–3. They held on for the next eleven minutes, and their come-from-behind victory tied the series at three games apiece.

"I thought we had the hockey game and we blew it," Reay said later. "We let in two goals on a couple of mistakes. We deserved to win and we didn't. It's an awful way to lose a hockey game. We seemed to have them on the hook today and we let 'em off."

So, after 97 games for the Canadiens (78 during the regular season plus 19 in the playoffs) and 95 for the Black Hawks, the whole 1970–71 campaign came down to one final match. The Hawks were favored, primarily because the game would be played in Chicago, but also because of lingering doubts that the MacNeil-Richard rift had indeed been healed. Publicly, the Canadiens were presenting a united front. Privately, well, no one could really tell.

When the teams took the ice for game number seven the temperature inside Chicago Stadium was in the low 80's. The ice was soft and the players obviously tense and tired. The game was being televised nationally in the United States by CBS. What millions of television viewers and the 20,000 fans in Chicago Stadium witnessed during 60 minutes of play was not hockey at its best, but certainly hockey at its most exciting.

From the opening face-off, Chicago carried the play. Only Ken Dryden prevented a Hawk runaway in that first period. First he stopped Stan Mikita at point-blank range with a kick save, and then moments later smothered a close-in follow shot by Eric Nesterenko. Later in the period he snaked out his long right leg to deflect a screen shot from the point by Keith Magnuson. Montreal, meanwhile, was having trouble getting organized. Esposito was tested, but not severely.

At 17:35 Rejean Houle was detected holding Bobby

Hull and sent to the penalty box for two minutes. With his team short-handed, Dryden stopped Jim Pappin on a close-in shot. Seconds later Bobby Hull fired a slapshot from the right point. Dryden used his stick to deflect it. When Hull's shot made contact with Dryden's stick it sounded like gunfire. Cliff Koroll captured the rebound and fed the puck back to Hull, still stationed at the right point. He unloaded again. Dryden went flopping across the crease to make sure he had the left-hand corner covered.

Hull's shot went wide but the puck rocketed off the boards behind the net and went straight to Dennis Hull, who was positioned in the left face-off circle. He shot as Dryden skidded back across the crease. The puck struck Dryden on the shoulder and glanced into the net. At 19:12 of the first period the Hawks had the lead.

Early in the second period, with the Hawks down two men and Montreal down one man, Montreal's Jacques Lemaire captured the puck five feet in front of Esposito and flipped a backhander for the corner. Somehow Esposito got his right leg out and blocked it. This seemed to inspire Chicago and for the next few minutes the Hawks swarmed around the Montreal net. Finally, after a face-off deep in Montreal ice, Chicago's Doug Jarrett shot the puck behind the net. Teammate Pit Martin outhustled two Canadiens for it and centered to Danny O'Shea. O'Shea fired from 25 feet out and the Hawks had a 2–0 lead. The game was nearly half over, and with Esposito in top form and the rest of the Hawks playing exceptionally well, it appeared that two goals would be enough for a Chicago win.

Then the roof fell in on the Black Hawks. Montreal got its first goal when Jacques Lemaire, skating leisurely toward the Chicago blue line, suddenly fired a slapshot toward the Chicago net from 80 feet out. Esposito flopped to his knees. But the puck kept rising and sailed over his right shoulder and into the net.

"I saw it all the way," Esposito said later. "I just missed it."

The goal stunned the Chicago crowd and the Chicago players as well. You could almost feel the confidence starting to drain out of them. Lemaire's goal came at 14:18.

Then at 18:20 the Canadiens tied the score. Chicago's Nesterenko and Lemaire chased the puck into the right corner of the Chicago zone. Nesterenko reached it first and tried to shoot it toward Bill White behind the Chicago goal. But the puck hit the side of the net and bounced back to Lemaire. He centered to Henri Richard and the "Pocket Rocket" fired the puck past Esposito at point-blank range. The Canadiens had come back again.

As the third period started there was a feeling of inevitability, the feeling that the Canadiens would not be denied. At 2:34 Henri Richard flashed across the Chicago blue line on the left side. Then, after eluding Magnuson, Richard got Esposito to drop to the ice and

The puck is in the net as Henri Richard scores the tying goal in the seventh game. Moments later he scored again to win the Cup.

flipped a shot over the sprawled goalie's shoulder. Montreal was ahead, 3–2, and now the game was in Dryden's hands.

Halfway through the third period, the young goalie made what has been described as "the stop of the season." Black Hawk Jim Pappin had taken a pass that left him in the clear eight feet in front of the Montreal net. He shot and then raised his stick in celebration, so certain was he that the puck was in.

"I was moving across the net, following the course of the pass," Dryden explained. "I really wasn't moving toward Pappin's shot. Pappin's shot hit me low on the right pad. I was fortunate."

Ten minutes later it was all over. The Canadiens had won their 16th Stanley Cup since the formation of the National Hockey League in 1917. It may have been the most satisfying Stanley Cup of all.

In the Montreal dressing room there was unrestrained joy. Some players were laughing, others were crying. Three of the Canadiens had hoisted MacNeil onto their shoulders and carried him off the ice. In the dressing room MacNeil and Richard embraced. All was forgiven in the flush of victory.

"This is my best ever," proclaimed Beliveau, "the one I enjoyed the most because we did what a lot of people didn't think we could do, beat the Bruins in Boston and the Hawks in Chicago."

"I am glad we won," Richard said. "It was a helluva relief after what I said the last time we were here. I should have kept my mouth shut. But I just lost my temper. It was one of those things I'll always be sorry for. Now maybe everybody will forget."

"Sure I was worried, but I had confidence, too," MacNeil said. "I was certain that they could win this seventh game in Chicago. These fellows are quite a hockey team."

Finally, Toe Blake, who had coached the Canadiens to eight Stanley Cup victories, said, "This is the greatest victory since I have been around the Canadiens. These fellows won every series on the other team's ice. That's an incredible feat, and they came from behind in several games, snatched victory from teams who thought they had won. No team has ever shown more heart under pressure."

When the Canadiens returned to Montreal in the early morning after their night of triumph, 3,000 fans were waiting to greet them. The next day a half-million Montrealers cheered their heroes during a motorcade from the Forum to City Hall. The biggest cheers were for Beliveau and Richard and for Dryden, who was awarded the Conn Smythe Trophy as the Most Valuable Player in the Stanley Cup playoffs.

There were cheers for Al MacNeil, too, but a few weeks later he was replaced as coach by Scotty Bowman, one-time coach and general-manager of the St. Louis Blues.

Ironically, the losing coach was more fortunate. Billy Reay was rehired because the Chicago management believed he was the man to win the Cup for the Black Hawks. Reay failed in 1972 when the Rangers wiped his Hawks out of the Cup semi-finals in four straight games. Then in 1972–73 the Chicagoans challenged again, meeting Montreal once more in the finals.

This time the Canadiens were favored. The World Hockey Association had changed the entire complexion of hockey, especially in Chicago. Bobby Hull, the

Three of the Montreal victors—Dryden, Beliveau and Frank Mahovlich—celebrate in the locker room.

mainstay of the Black Hawks for 15 years, had signed a ten-year $2,750,000 contract to play and coach for the Winnipeg Jets.

By contrast, the Canadiens had suffered no significant defections to the WHA and appeared as strong as they had been in 1971. This time Montreal won the first two games at home. The Hawks rallied for a 7–4 triumph in Chicago, but lost the fourth game 4–0. The Hawks enjoyed their final gasp on May 8, 1973, in a wild, virtually defenseless game at Montreal, winning 8–7. Neither goalie earned any praise from that one but at least the Chicagoans were alive for the sixth game on their home ice.

When the last ice chip had fallen, Montreal skated off with the big trophy along with the 6–4 win. The difference between the two teams was the same as it had been a decade earlier when the roots of the rivalry had been planted. The Canadiens had too much class, too much pride.

"We had to win," said captain Henri Richard. "After finishing first our fans expected us to win the Cup. When you are the Canadiens you cannot make excuses."

Before the 1973–74 season, the Black Hawks lost two more of their top players when defenseman Pat Stapleton and center Ralph Backstrom jumped to the WHA. But the Canadiens lost their goalie, Ken Dryden, when he decided to sit out the season. Both teams lost their top positions in regular-season play and were eliminated in the early rounds of the playoffs. Many observers felt that the great Black Hawk–Canadien rivalry had come to an end.

Bobby Orr
vs.
Brad Park

It was early in the evening of January 25, 1972, at Metropolitan Sports Center in Bloomington, Minnesota. The cream of the National Hockey League crop began drifting into the East Division dressing room for the annual East-West All-Star Game.

For one evening, at least, all hatreds between opponents were to be suspended. Vic Hadfield of the New York Rangers joked with Phil Esposito of the Boston Bruins. Frank Mahovlich of the Montreal Canadiens enjoyed a pleasant conversation with Paul Henderson of the Toronto Maple Leafs. It was a lovely truce among the ice warriors—except for one corner of the room where First All-Star defenseman Brad Park of the Rangers unloaded his gear.

At the time Park, a chunky, baby-faced hitter who was affectionately known as "Huckleberry Finn on Skates," was rated second to the other First All-Star defenseman, Bobby Orr of the Bruins. Blond, handsome and as tough as Park, Orr often was regarded as the greatest hockey player of all time.

The warmth that surrounded Mahovlich, Esposito, Henderson and Hadfield stopped short of Park's cubicle. One observer remarked that when he approached Park he could cut the tension with a knife. "The temperature was 30 below zero outside the rink," said hockey writer Red Burnett of The Toronto *Star*, "and the air around Park in the dressing room when Esposito, Orr and Johnny McKenzie of the Bruins went past him was 50-below and dropping."

Significantly, Esposito, Orr and McKenzie all skated for the Bruins, a club which had been mauling the Rangers for decades. Orr, a native of Parry Sound, a village in Northern Ontario, had entered the NHL with a blaring fanfare in 1966 and then proceeded to demolish nearly all the records held by defensemen as if the job were child's play.

By contrast, Park quietly became a big-leaguer two years after Orr's entrance. Several months elapsed before the Rangers' defenseman began to be recognized as one of the game's greatest. From the beginning Brad was Number Two, but he did try harder and his perseverance paid handsome dividends. By the start of the 1971–72 season he not only was being favorably compared with the gifted Orr but a few critics rated him even better than Bobby.

"Park is defensively sounder than Orr" said Detroit Red Wings manager Ned Harkness. "Brad's a great one. By comparison, Orr is more offensive-minded."

Vancouver Canucks executive Hal Laycoe who once played for both Boston and New York, also favored

Bobby Orr: "the greatest hockey player of all time."

Park over Orr and predicted that the Rangers' defenseman would outlast the Bruins ace because Orr is more susceptible to injury. "Park is tough and aggressive," said Laycoe. "He's likely to have a longer and more productive career than Orr."

Although Park, himself, had suffered injuries as a young player, Orr's gimpy knees were regarded as the problem that could abruptly end his career at any moment. Yet Orr continued to play a free-wheeling game, frequently carrying the puck from one end of the rink to the other and setting up forwards or scoring goals himself. Park, too, could skate with power and speed but Brad's strong hand was his ability to manipulate the puck in and around his skates with a magical "now-you-see-it-now-you-don't" quality. Having outwitted the enemy with his adroit stickhandling, Park usually would pass the puck to a free wingman or his fellow defenseman. Then he'd skate to the opponent's blue line and await a potential return pass for a hard shot on goal. Both Park and Orr both could fire shots of more than 100 miles per hour.

So in January 1972 Park and Orr were virtually equals as performers. But others in that All-Star group were equally talented at their positions. Why should there have been a special rivalry between Orr and Park?

The answer was that the Ranger ace had carried his battle against Orr and the Bruins out of the playing area. The Boston players wanted to freeze out the New York defenseman because they believed that Park had

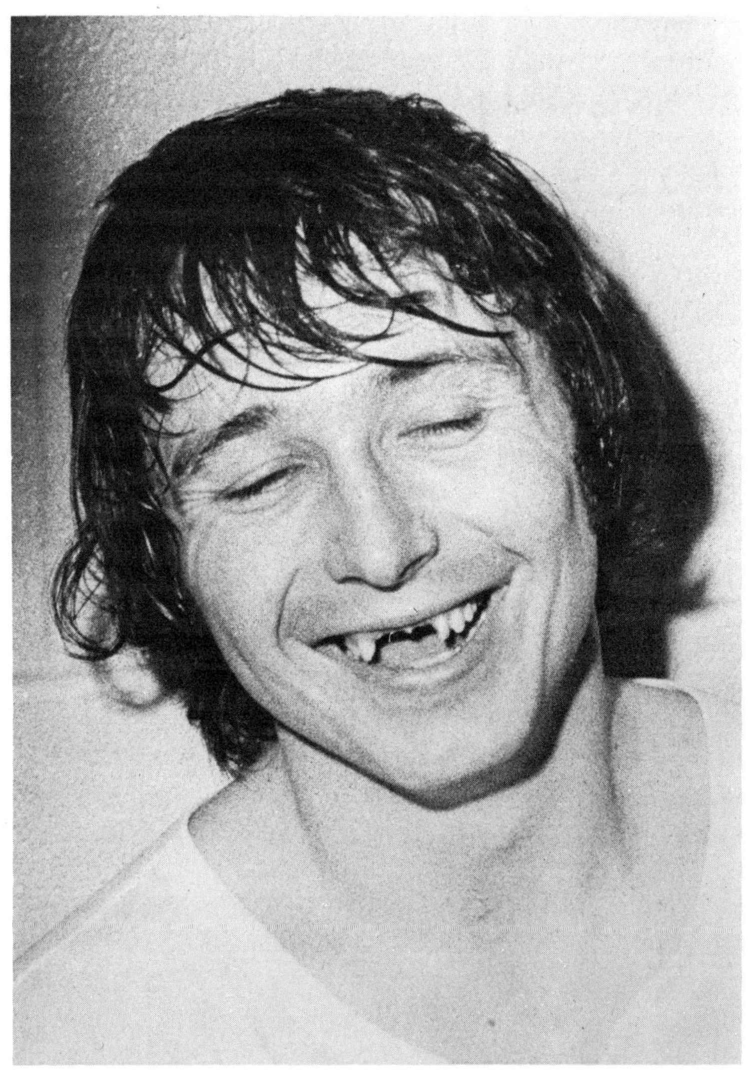

Brad Park: a toothless victory smile after beating the Bruins.

burned them as a team and particularly Orr in print.

The Bruins had just read Park's autobiography, *Play the Man*, and bubbled with anger over statements Brad had made about Orr. "I hated sharing the dressing room with that creep," said Orr's teammate and friend Johnny McKenzie. "Park's presence took all the joy out of being an All-Star."

What angered Orr and his teammates were Brad's words on page 67 of his book: "Orr doesn't like to get hit, and sometimes he'll throw a cheap shot at one of our guys. A man of his ability needn't revert to such stuff, but he does."

Park's anti-Orr barrage set off explosions throughout the NHL. One headline shouted: "BRUINS ARE BUSH, BRAD PARK WRITES." Another alluded to Park's concern about retaliation: "AUTHOR EXPECTS TO BE A MARKED MAN."

No doubt Park was a marked man in the All-Stars' dressing room, but once on the ice that night he was promised a temporary truce by Orr and his Boston friends. Park responded by skimming a perfect pass to McKenzie late in the second period, enabling the Bruin to tie the game. Phil Espositio scored in the final period to give the East team a 3–2 edge over the West Division stars. But once the match had ended the truce melted in the heat of anger. Park became a marked man in both Boston Garden and his own Madison Square Garden whenever the Rangers and Bruins played.

The Bruins had the toughness—and some said the

meanness—to retaliate against Park. "They're not called 'The Big, Bad Bruins' for nothing," said former NHL defenseman Carl Brewer. "Boston has brutalized the game of hockey. On the other hand, Park plays the game hard but clean, the way it's supposed to be played."

Park was right. The Bruins were rough and often dirty. Orr frequently would erupt in anger even if cleanly hit. More often, revenge was left to his teammates. Once when Toronto defenseman Pat Quinn nailed Bobby with a legal bodycheck, it appeared that the entire Boston team would try to assassinate Quinn.

"The Bruins," said former NHL forward Brian Conacher, "like the gang-warfare style of hockey. And they have the guys to play that kind of nasty game."

Unfortunately for Park, his Rangers were not equipped for Boston's heavy body play and angry stick-swinging. Park and clean-playing center Jean Ratelle epitomized the New Yorkers' Boy Scout style of hockey. It all made Brad's battle against Orr and his Bruin mates that much more difficult.

In Boston Garden, Orr's army of fans deafened Park with hostile barbs whenever he stepped on the ice. But the young Ranger shrugged off the boos and played his usual competent game. "They never loved me in Boston anyway," Park explained, "so it shouldn't have made much difference. Anyway, I'm not paid to like people. What I said in the book about Orr and the Bruins describes the way I feel."

Orr, himself, rarely took on Park either physically or verbally. But his teammates were plenty willing. Both Johnny McKenzie and Ted Green went after Brad and, each time, Park punished them with a flurry of punches. Nevertheless, the Bruins kept coming back, determined, it seemed, to edit Park's "heretic" book on the ice. And yet Park continued to tear away at Orr's image.

"One of the myths of hockey," said Park, "is that Orr is unstoppable. Some people have written, and rightly so, that Orr can be held in tow by forechecking him in his own end of the rink before he has a chance to get up a head of steam, and by taking advantage of the big openings he leaves when he takes off on one of his many rushes into enemy territory."

Such barbs continued to peck away at Orr's ego. But Bobby refused to reply in kind. Time and again newspapermen attempted to get Bobby to answer, but he played the questions as coolly as he would intercept an enemy forward on the ice. "I'll do my talking during the games," he insisted.

Brad seemed to revel in the controversy. "Somebody called me an egotist," he said, "but heck, the book is *my* book." While Park talked endlessly with newsmen, Bobby would frequently hide in the privacy of the Bruins' trainer's room to avoid the questioners. When Orr was cornered, he would duck the direct answer to a direct question.

"I never think of myself as an idol," said Orr. "I'm a hockey player. I enjoy hockey. The money? I never think about becoming a millionaire, or anything like that. When I quit hockey, it will be because I don't enjoy it any more."

"Throughout it all," said author Tom Dowling, "Orr remains remote and circumspect, a little abashed at all the furor unloosed in his name."

Perhaps Park's literary onslaught would have been casually ignored by Orr had Brad been a mediocre player. But the Ranger was the prince, if not king, of defensemen. More than that, he seemed to have obtained a keen insight into the Orr style, one which apparently eluded many viewers.

"Another myth about Orr," Park went on, "is that he's a gentlemanly and clean player. Actually, Orr can be a hatchetman just like some of his Boston teammates. This makes opponents more wary of him. Sometimes Bobby pulls off the cheap shots that really aren't necessary under any conditions."

As the Park-Orr feud worsened in the 1970s, observers wondered just what kept prompting Park to explode with so many headline-grabbing statements that infuriated some of Brad's own teammates as well as the Bruins. "I said what I felt," Park insisted. "I'm not paid to love the Bruins nor their fans. I know that what I've said arouses them. And I'm sure they are more interested in seeing me get licked than anything else. It's all part of the game."

Some thought that Park spoke out because he did not receive the recognition he thought he deserved. It was easy for Orr to be a well-known hockey superstar

Park fights for the puck with the Bruins' Phil Esposito.

in Boston, which is the most avid hockey town outside of Canada. But it was more difficult for Park to be a hero in giant New York City where hockey often is a stepchild to the more popular basketball and where celebrities from all fields seem to be a dime a dozen. Even after Park had reached the heights in his profession he still was hardly recognized off the ice in his team's hometown.

"Stop people on the streets of New York," noted *Sports Illustrated*, "and ask them about Brad Park, and the answers will sometimes be confusing. Brad Park is a playground in The Bronx. Brad Park is a botanical garden over in Brooklyn. Brad Park is a garage near the 59th Street Bridge.

"But mention that name on Ste. Catherine Street in Montreal or on Boylston Street in Boston. 'Brad Park,' goes the response, 'is Bobby Orr disguised as a New York Ranger.' "

Even the Boston fans came to appreciate Park's fighting spirit. Whenever the Bruins would attempt to bully the Rangers, Park seemed to arrive on the scene, ready and willing to take on all comers. Twice during the 1971–72 season Park tangled with Bruin players on Boston ice. Each time Brad so thoroughly outpointed the home skater that a second Bruin was compelled to intrude and save his teammate.

One time when Park was fighting McKenzie, one of his favorite Boston targets, Phil Esposito, rushed in to rescue his mate. Surprisingly, Park approved. "Esposito is a terrific team man," said Brad. "He stepped in when it looked like McKenzie and I were going toe-to-toe. I'm a few inches taller and heavier, and logically, I should take McKenzie . . . so Espo came into it. A good team man does something like that."

No matter what he did, Park still couldn't obtain recognition throughout the NHL that he was superior to Orr. A few critics thought so, but even some of Brad's friends admitted the opinion that Bobby was better. "Brad is a very good defenseman," said Harry Howell, who once teamed with Park on the New York defense. "Second to Orr. Bobby is the best I've ever seen."

"I don't mind being Number Two," Park insisted. "It's a challenge. If I think the guy is better than me, I have to try harder. If I work harder, I play better—better than anybody."

Translating the words to action was not always easy. Two months after Orr and Park had confronted one another at the 1972 All-Star Game they met again at Boston Garden. This time the Bruins won the match 8–1. Park played capably, to be sure, but his teammates appeared lost. Many of the Rangers privately complained that Brad's book had done them as much harm as the Boston sticks.

"There's no doubt," agreed Bruins executive Tom Johnson, "that Park's book helped us more than it's helped the Rangers. It gave our guys extra incentive to beat them. I wonder, though, if Brad even realizes how much the things he said in the book can hurt him and the Rangers. He's certainly entitled to his opinions, but he's lost respect among his fellow players for the things he wrote."

Brad had expected to antagonize Orr and the Bruins but he never expected hostile reactions from his own buddies. After that 8–1 shellacking a newspaperman approached Brad and began asking him questions. Ranger star Rod Gilbert leaned over and quipped sarcastically, "Go ahead, Brad, and tell him something that will make another team mad at us. We haven't got enough people sore at us now."

Orr's Bruins ultimately finished first in the East Division in the 1971–72 season, ten points ahead of Park's Rangers. Bobby also topped Brad in scoring—117 points to 49. But the New Yorkers would get their opportunity for revenge in the 1972 Stanley Cup finals.

The 1972 Stanley Cup collision marked the high point of the Boston–New York rivalry. It was the first time that the two foes had met in the finals since 1929. The natural competition between the teams was even further inflamed by Park's comments, which by this time had been so well-circulated they were on the lips of fans from Boston to Bangor.

The Bruins were leading in the opening game, 5–1, when the Rangers made a miraculous comeback to tie the match, 5–5, in the third period. With such momentum in their favor the visiting New Yorkers seemed certain to go on to victory. Then Ace Bailey went on an end run with the puck. Only Brad and Ranger goaltender Ed Giacomin were between him and the goal. Bailey skated one-on-one with Park, and Brad attempted to steer him into a corner where he would be helpless with the puck.

"I thought I had him," said Park.

But he didn't. To the great glee of the Boston

Garden rooters, Bailey sliced around Park and flipped the puck over the fallen goalie Ed Giacomin. It happened with only 2:16 remaining in the third period and Boston won, 6–5.

The Bruins won the second game, and then the series moved to New York. In the third contest, on friendly Madison Square Garden ice, Park took command. He dazzled the Bruins with his stickwork and personally led the Rangers to their first victory, a 5–2 decision. He played defense as if there were a net hung across the Ranger blue line. Time and again, he set teammates in motion with pinpoint passes, and even scored one goal himself.

With Boston leading the best-of-seven series two games to one, most experts believed that the fourth game would be decisive. If Park could orchestrate another Ranger victory, New York might have a chance to win its first Stanley Cup in 32 years.

Never was the Orr-Park rivalry more intense. Whenever possible, Bruins Wayne Cashman, Ken Hodge and Phil Esposito took dead aim at Park and battered him with their bodies. Heroically, Brad fended them off, waiting for Orr to enter the fray. When he did, early in the game, Brad was ready. He dropped his gloves; so did Orr. In a flash the two superstars flailed away at each other, connecting with left and right jabs. They fell to the ice in a heap with Orr on top and neither was able to gain a clear-cut victory. But Orr was on top in the skating and shooting department that afternoon, and the Bruins bested the Rangers, 3–2.

The rivals: Brad and Bobby in 1972.

Neither Park nor his teammates were ready to throw in the towel. They returned to Beantown and scratched out a 3–2 victory over the Bruins. But the Bruins' incessant pounding had taken its toll on Park's body. In the sixth game, without any beefy teammates to help him, Brad fought off the enemy for nearly two periods and tried to direct the Rangers attack and defense at the same time.

With no score early in the game, Bobby Orr directed a Boston power play into New York territory. Bruce

MacGregor attempted to stop him at the blue line but Bobby did a reverse swivel and got away. Then he released a sizzling shot that blurred past goalie Gilles Villemure.

The Bruins nursed their 1–0 lead into the second period when Park enjoyed a great opportunity to tie the match. Boston goalie Gerry Cheevers had been caught out of his net, giving Brad the entire four-by-six-foot goal at which to shoot. Instead of firing immediately, Park hesitated. By the time he shot, Bruin defenseman Don Awrey was in front of the yawning cage. Awrey sprawled and deflected the puck harmlessly to the side.

New York continued to persist, chasing the 1–0 deficit. Park played well but Orr played better. In the third period Bobby took a pass from Phil Esposito and drilled a shot that whistled through a maze of legs, then off Wayne Cashman's stick into the net. That took the wind out of the Rangers' sails. The Bruins scored again, and minutes later, they danced with joy, having won the game, 3–0, and the Stanley Cup.

Nobody was more downhearted or bitter about the loss than Park. When the skaters lined up at center ice for the traditional post-game handshaking ceremonies Park was reluctant to take part. "I thought I just couldn't line up and shake hands with them," he said. "I was turning to go straight to the dressing room. Then, I saw Orr at the front of the line. I changed my mind. I have tremendous respect for him."

But the Orr–Park rivalry was far from over. Before

the 1972–73 season began, Orr had an operation on one of his bad knees. He returned for the 1972–73 campaign a slower skater than before, and it appeared that Park might finally become the Number One defenseman.

Like many Orr-watchers, Park noticed the change in Bobby's style. And once again, he couldn't keep his mouth shut. "Last year," he said, "when Bobby hit our blue line he was accelerating. Now he's just moving regularly when he hits the line. What that means is that we—the defensemen—can angle Orr against the boards because he does not have the spurt to go around us."

But Park got his come-uppance in November 1972 when his bad knee was injured in a collision with Philadelphia defenseman Ed Van Impe. Another collision a month later worsened the condition, and Park lost a step in the process.

"I had to readjust my style because of it," Brad admitted. "It was frustrating. I could take a full stride with the left leg but only a half stride with the right; it gave me a gimpy effect. I couldn't rely on my reflexes enough. I had to out-think guys coming at me, try to head them off at the pass. And if I made a mistake, I couldn't always recover quick enough and too often the guy was gone."

Even with the injuries, Park and Orr stood head and shoulders above other defensemen most of the time and led their teams into a head-to-head confrontation once more in the playoffs. "Our Day Will Come," sang

Park before the opening face-off and, this time, he was right.

Although the series opened on Boston Garden ice, Park never was better and the Rangers seemed to take heart from his performance. Pushing the Bruins aside as if they were plastic table hockey players, the Rangers stunned Boston with a 6–2 defeat and followed that with a 4–2 decision. After two games at home, the mighty Bruins were down two games to none.

Oddly enough, the Bruins came to life in New York in the third game, winning 4–2. But it had become apparent that Orr could be stopped, and when Orr was stopped the Bruins were dead.

"We watched films of Orr in action," said Rangers goalie Ed Giacomin. "After studying the films we decided that the best way to keep him from hurting us was to flood his side. We kept throwing the puck in and making him go back and chase it. If that's done to anyone, the player will get tired. That's what happened to Orr, and it hurt his game."

This was obvious in the fifth game of the series, at Boston. Orr moved as if he were skating in mud while Park flitted around the rink as if he had wings on his boots. The Rangers easily won the match, 6–3, and eliminated the Bruins.

Park unquestionably was the hero, outplaying Orr in every phase of the game, including Bobby's forte, scoring. In the five games, Park collected two goals and four assists for six points, right behind team leader Bill Fairbairn who had eight points. Virtually helpless against the New York defenses, Orr managed only one goal and one assist.

That round went to Park, but Orr was heard from again in May 1973 when the All-Star ballots were counted. The votes kept the Bruins star on top, giving him a spot on the First Team for the sixth consecutive year. Park, who had been a First All-Star twice, was relegated to the Second Team.

From all indications "Number Two" would remain second-best to Orr as long as Bobby's knees were able to carry him at top speed.

Inge Hammarstrom of the Toronto Maple Leafs, who had played in the top European leagues against the foremost Russian, Czechoslovak and Finnish aces, summed up the majority opinion about the Orr–Park argument. "There are many stars, fine skaters, stick-handlers and playmakers and scorers," said Hammarstrom, "but none can control an entire game like Orr. He amazes you the way he sets the tempo of a game from fast to slow and back again."

In 1973–74 Bobby led the Bruins back to the top of the East Divison while Park's Rangers remained in close pursuit. The two defensemen had matured considerably since their early days in the majors. Both had married. Both had emerged as the unquestioned leaders of their respective teams and were counted among the most exciting personalities in hockey history.

4
SHER-WOOD

If Orr kept his edge over Park on the ice, Park remained the more colorful of the two as he continued to strive for the coveted Number One position.

"Brad knows that Bobby is the greatest player *at the moment*," said a close friend of Park's. "But he also knows that if Orr's knees ever go, the best defenseman in the world will be Brad Park. In the meantime Brad remains the best-selling defenseman-author."

That was true. Meanwhile, the bitterness was still evident whenever Brad encountered the Bruins. "It happens whenever the Rangers play the Bruins," said Hugh Delano of The New York *Post* during the 1973–74 season. "The Bruins fans won't let the Rangers' defenseman forget their anger at what he wrote about their heroes."

So, as long as there is a Brad Park skating for New York and a Bobby Orr for Boston the rivalry will flame, all because a young defenseman decided to turn author—a defenseman who has no regrets, just bruises where the Bruins have hit him year after year.

"Everything I put in the book," said Park, "reflected the way I felt. I have no regrets about it. After all, I can't say everybody's a good guy."

Then, a pause and a wink: "But I'll say that Bobby Orr is a great hockey player. Maybe even better than me!"

The amazing Bobby Orr, far from his defenseman's position, drives in to score.

Detroit Red Wings
vs.
Toronto Maple Leafs

One of the most intense feuds in National Hockey League history was conducted between two of the most determined and accomplished teams the game has known, the Detroit Red Wings and the Toronto Maple Leafs of the 1940s and early '50s.

A seemingly endless period of competition between Toronto and Detroit began in 1942 in the Stanley Cup finals. Coached by Hap Day, the Maple Leafs were one of the traditionally strong teams in the league, and they were heavily favored in the best-of-seven series against Detroit. Imagine their surprise when they lost three straight games to the Red Wings and appeared destined for a humiliating four-straight wipe-out. No team had ever lost the first three and come back to win.

In a brutal fourth game, however, the Leafs regained their composure and the Red Wings lost theirs.

Detroit's rotund manager Jack Adams was renowned for his tantrums, but during that fourth contest he outdid himself. In the closing moments, with Detroit hopelessly behind, Adams leaped over the sideboards to challenge a decision of referee Mel Harwood. Adams underlined his points by tossing a series of punches at Harwood until the linesmen pulled him away. NHL president Frank Calder suspended Adams for the rest of the playoffs, and many observers thought that Adams' explosion so disrupted his team that his players no longer could concentrate on their task.

Whatever the reason, Detroit fell apart completely and Toronto won the next three games and the Cup. The Red Wings were humiliated. Some Detroit supporters insisted that the league president had been too hard on manager Adams, and the bitterness between the two teams smoldered long after the series was over. The Leafs–Red Wings rivalry had been born.

Canada had been at war since 1939, and in late 1941 the United States entered the war, too. A growing number of hockey players were disappearing from the NHL to serve in the armed forces, and the hockey picture became odd and unpredictable. Many young, inexperienced players arrived to replace departing stars and a few of them became history-making stars themselves. In 1942–43 a young Maurice Richard first skated for Montreal.

And late that same season another youngster appeared in a Toronto uniform who was destined to be the focus of the bitter rivalry with Detroit. His name was Ted Kennedy. In his first workout with the NHL club, Kennedy won a rave from the Toronto *Telegram*'s hockey writer who described him as a "big, upstanding sort of lad with a fair turn of speed and a good shot."

Kennedy played only two games in the tail end of the 1942–43 season. He had been suffering a groin injury and was benched for the playoffs. "To keep up his morale," said acting Leaf manager Frank Selke, "I

Young Ted Kennedy (left) gets the puck for the Maple Leafs.

had him sit with me, and I was dumbfounded by his mature observations on the game as it progressed. I remember telling sportswriter Ed Fitkin that I thought we might have acquired a superstar."

Kennedy did become a Toronto regular but almost by default. He had been well schooled in hockey basics, but he was weak in one department: skating. His strides were labored, almost painful to watch, and he moved like an express train with some of its wheels locked. But the armed forces had claimed such aces as Billy Taylor, Sweeney Schriner, Syl Apps and Turk Broda. Kennedy played alongside other promising youngsters such as forward Gus Bodnar and defenseman Elwyn "Moe" Morris. "It appears," said coach Hap Day, "that we have reached the Children's Hour in the NHL." Looking forward to 1943–44, he added, "We may be short on ability, but I think we're going to be long on action."

There was plenty of action on the Toronto roster cards. Because of the war, some players arrived and others departed almost every week. One Maple Leaf goaltender that year was Benny Grant, who last played goal for the Maple Leafs as a substitute between 1929 and 1932.

Still, the Leafs played sensationally. Their first game was on October 30, 1943, against the Rangers at Maple Leaf Gardens. Rookie Gus Bodnar scored only fifteen seconds into the game, and Ted Kennedy closed out the Maple Leafs' scoring that night, as Toronto won 5–2.

Despite his labored skating, Kennedy's perseverance and grim determination soon gained the attention of Maple Leaf fans. A service station operator named John Arnott noticed particularly. He had become famous for his penetrating cheers directed at Leaf star Pete Langelle. During a lull in the action Arnott would develop a slow crescendo, imploring, "C'monnn, P-E-T-E-R!" But Langelle was in the army, so Arnott had no one special to cheer for.

Then one night Arnott became enthralled with young Ted Kennedy. Just as a face-off was about to take place, a booming voice could be heard across Maple Leaf Gardens. "C'monnnn, T-E-E-D-E-R!" A new hero was born in Toronto.

"He hadn't intended to let out that yell," wrote Ed Fitkin in his biography of Kennedy, *C'mon Teeder!* "It sort of slipped out accidentally. But at the same time he realized that here, at last, was the only type of player who could take Pete Langelle's place in his affection. . . . To Arnott, Kennedy was the greatest competitive player in the NHL."

Teeder finished his freshman season with 26 goals and 23 assists for 49 points. (It was a high-scoring year because there were so many inept goaltenders.) The Maple Leafs finished third of six teams in the league.

Toronto and Detroit did not meet again in the Stanley Cup playoffs until the spring of 1945. Three years after the famous '42 series the Red Wings and Maple Leafs collided in the championship round once again.

This time the Red Wings were heavy favorites. They had finished the regular season 15 points ahead of the Maple Leafs. But Teeder Kennedy and his teammates weren't worried. Although the war was still going on, and players were hard to come by, the Leafs had found a goalie—a thin, nervous man named Frank McCool. In the first two games at Detroit, McCool blanked the Red Wings twice—1–0 and 2–0. Then in game three at Maple Leaf Gardens he came up with his third straight shutout, 1–0. Three consecutive shutouts in a Stanley Cup final!

The Red Wings were down. "It doesn't look like the puck ever is going to go in for us," snapped Jack Adams. But the Detroiters finally broke their scoring drought in the fourth game at 8:35 of the first period. The Leafs needed only to win the game to take the Stanley Cup, and they counterattacked. Teeder Kennedy scored a three-goal hat trick and put Toronto ahead early in the third period, but the Red Wings weren't finished. Sparked by rookie left wing Ted Lindsay, Detroit rallied for a 5–3 victory.

In the fifth game Detroit came out on top 2–0. Now they had two wins to Toronto's three. Red Wing fans began to believe that maybe their team could get revenge for 1942 by winning four straight as Toronto had done. The sixth game was a heart-stopper. Both McCool and Detroit goalie Harry Lumley practiced the art of netminding to perfection that night. In 60 minutes, neither team could score, so the contest went into sudden-death overtime.

In the 15th minute of overtime, Harold Jackson of Detroit blooped a high shot into Maple Leaf territory that bounced off the wire netting behind and to one side of the goal. It seemed to be out of the danger zone, and Maple Leaf goalie Frank McCool seemed unconcerned. But the puck must have struck the netting at a crazy angle because it caromed back into play with unusual force, falling in front of the net. Ed Bruneteau of Detroit was there, and he easily pushed the puck past McCool.

The final game would be played in Detroit, and if the Red Wings could win, they could claim the Stanley Cup.

Detroit fans were already exultant. But Toronto coach Hap Day called a team meeting. "I see by the Detroit papers," said Day, "that we are about to get beaten. I don't believe it, and I hope you don't believe it. Show me a game like you did the other night in Toronto and we'll win the Cup."

The Leafs got an early goal from Mel Hill, and Frank McCool—whose job caused him to suffer from ulcers—held the Red Wings scoreless into the third period. If only McCool could pull off one more shutout, Toronto fans were thinking. But then at 8:16 of the third period Detroit's Murray Armstrong scored on a rebound shot. The game was tied.

The momentum should have shifted to the Red Wings, but it didn't. Two minutes later referee Bill Chadwick whistled Syd Howe of the Red Wings into the penalty box for high-sticking Gus Bodnar. Toronto's Hap Day immediately sent his power play out for the kill. Babe Pratt passed the puck from the blue line to Nick Metz, who was standing in front of the net. Metz shot, but goaltender Harry Lumley anticipated the move and blocked it. The rebound skimmed out to the onrushing Babe Pratt, who fired it into the net. For the next eight minutes McCool filled the net as never before. Toronto won the game, 2–1, and the Stanley Cup. The Leafs had round two of the running rivalry, but Detroit had given them a bad scare once again.

Teeder Kennedy was the toast of Toronto, having led the playoffs in goal-scoring with seven. "There are few great hockey players in the NHL today," wrote Andy Lytle in the Toronto *Daily Star*. "Kennedy is assuredly and emphatically one of them."

Sitting dolefully in the Red Wing dressing room was a young left wing who hated to lose. Ted Lindsay had been born to be a hockey player. His father, Bert Lindsay, had been a first-rate goalie at the turn of the century and played alongside such legendary aces as Newsy Lalonde, Lester Patrick and Cyclone Taylor. Ted Lindsay had arrived at the Red Wings' training camp in the fall of 1944, an unknown among 63 skaters auditioning for the NHL club. But in no time at all he was discovered by manager Adams.

"There's a kid after my own heart," said Adams. "Look at the way he steps into those big guys."

Lindsay had played his first game for the Red Wings on October 29, 1944, and helped Detroit to a 7–1 victory over the Chicago Black Hawks. In his second game he scored his first NHL goals as the Red Wings trounced the New York Rangers, 10–3.

"I knew he had a lot of moxie," said Adams, "and I knew he'd do a good job. But he has exceeded anything I had hoped for. Lindsay is just a natural. He is going to be one of the really great ones in the NHL."

Adams was right. Within two years Lindsay was teamed with Gordie Howe and Sid Abel to comprise the great "Production Line" of Detroit. By the 1946–47 season they appeared ready to make a formidable bid for the Stanley Cup—except for the interference of Ted Kennedy's Maple Leafs.

In the opening round of the 1947 playoff, Toronto eliminated Detroit in five games. A season later they met in the Cup finals and, this time, the Leafs walloped Detroit in four consecutive games. Kennedy led all skaters in playoff scoring. The Red Wings' wounds were getting deeper.

In 1948–49 Toronto still further aggravated the worsening relations between the teams, once again wiping Detroit out of the finals, four games to none! Kennedy and Lindsay finished in a second-place tie for scoring. But now the Leafs had beaten their rivals in the playoffs five times in eight years. And they had won the last eleven games in a row.

All of this led to the 1950 Cup playoffs. The Leafs and the Red Wings met in the first round. (In those days there were only six NHL teams; four qualified for the first playoff round and the two winners met for the championship in the second round.) It was hardly

Detroit's pugnacious Ted Lindsay.

surprising that a feeling of imminent warfare hung over Detroit's Olympia Stadium before the first game of the series on March 28, 1950. Once again, Kennedy was spotlighted as the most important Toronto player. The Red Wings had Gordie Howe, who was becoming the greatest all-round player in history, clever Sid Abel, and intense, combative Ted Lindsay. Seldom had hockey seen such a line.

"Barring injuries," said Jack Adams, "we can do it. We've got the team this year." The significant word turned out to be "injuries," and an injury in the very first game would make this series one of the most controversial ever played.

Before the opening face-off referee George Gravel, who was something of a cut-up, attempted to lighten the scene by bowing deeply from the waist in the direction of the press box. The crowd may have been amused, but the players were grim. A fight erupted early in the first period between Marty Pavelich and Fleming Mackell. Another, involving Gordie Howe and Bill Juzda, exploded soon after. Both quarrels were ended by the officials without serious consequences, however. By the middle of the third period, Toronto had coasted to a 4–0 lead. The game seemed out of reach, and Detroit fans assumed that the Wings would calmly skate out the final minutes, conserving their energies (and their anger) for the second game.

Then the Leafs' Teeder Kennedy got the puck and sidestepped his way across the Leaf blue line on a down-ice sweep. Kennedy was six feet from the left boards as he reached center ice. Behind him in hot pursuit was Red Wing defenseman Jack Stewart. Sweeping in from the right side was Howe, who attempted to crash Kennedy amidships. Howe was skating a trifle too slowly to hit Kennedy with full force, and it appeared that the best he might do would be to graze the Leaf and throw him off balance. Then Kennedy stopped short. With nothing to check, Howe flew in front of Kennedy and tumbled, face first, into the thick wooden sideboards. Kennedy tripped over Howe and went down, too. Seconds later, action was stopped as Howe was lying unconscious on the ice, his face covered with blood. As 13,659 fans sat, horror-struck, Gordie Howe, their greatest player, was carried off the ice on a stretcher and removed to Harper Hospital.

For several hours there was doubt that he would survive. His skull was fractured and brain damage was feared. A call was put through to Saskatoon, Saskatchewan, to urge Gordie's mother to take the first plane to Detroit so that she could be at her son's bedside. But Gordie pulled through. Two days later, when Mrs. Howe got in from Saskatchewan, she told reporters, "He still has a headache, but he's feeling fine."

But Detroit's press and public were not listening. As far as they were concerned, Gordie had been lethally assaulted and somebody would have to pay for it. Toronto naturally denied responsibility for Howe's injury, and the argument raged like a forest fire.

The story in the Detroit papers was that Teeder

Kennedy had deliberately speared Howe. Kennedy offered to take an oath that he had not caused the injury. "I saw Howe lying on the ice with his face covered with blood," said the Leaf captain, "and I couldn't help thinking what a great player he was and how I hoped he wasn't badly hurt. Then Detroit players started saying I did it with my stick. I knew I hadn't, and as I've always regarded coach Tommy Ivan as a sensible, level-headed man, I went over to the Detroit bench and told him I was sorry Howe was hurt but that I wasn't responsible."

His Red Wing teammates carry the injured Gordie Howe off the ice on a stretcher during the 1950 playoffs against Toronto.

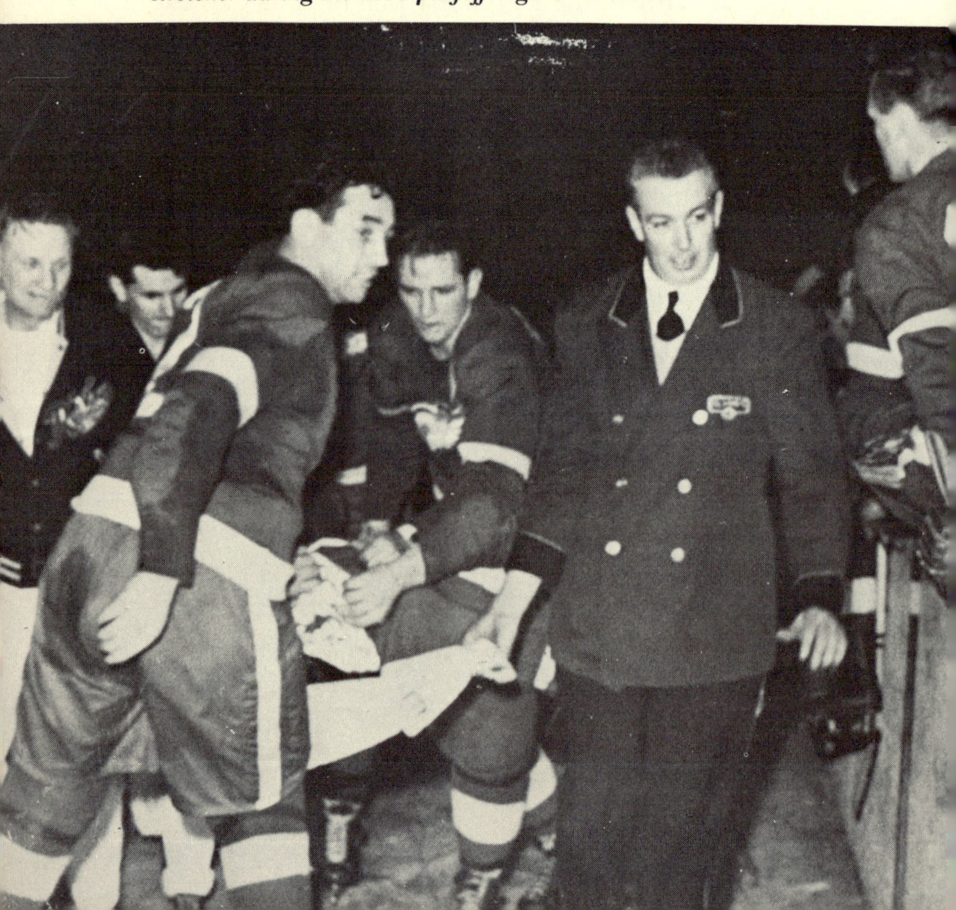

Al Nickleson, who covered the game for the Toronto *Globe and Mail*, wrote: "It appeared to this observer that Kennedy, in stopping short, had raised his elbow as a protective gesture and that Howe had struck it, before smashing into the boards with his face as he fell."

NHL President Clarence Campbell was blamed in Detroit for his failure to prevent the brutality and violence that preceded Howe's injury. But Campbell quickly took a stand on the Howe case. He made it clear that game officials had absolved Kennedy of any blame for Howe's injury, and he branded as "very vicious" the charge of Tommy Ivan, manager of the Red Wings, that Kennedy had "butt-ended" Howe on the play. Kennedy, he declared, could not possibly have fouled Howe in that way.

"Kennedy," said Campbell, "as a right-handed player, had the butt part of his stick tight to the fence as he was going up the ice. He was being checked from his right. The injuries to Howe were on the right side of the head. Kennedy had stopped to avoid the check, and Howe went in front of him."

Toronto owner Conn Smythe stood behind Kennedy, too. "It seems that every time the Leafs go out to defend the championship, they have to defend their right to play," he said. "Loose accusations against players have no place in the game. Neither has rough hockey. Kennedy always has been a great and clean player. . . ."

But whatever the facts of the case, it was clear that

Toronto goalie Turk Broda comes far out of the net to make a save on Detroit's Jeff Cravath during the 1950 playoffs.

the rest of the series would be played with an intensity and bitterness seldom seen even in hockey. Even before that first game ended, Ted Kennedy had been slashed across the ankle by the stick of Sid Abel, Gordie Howe's linemate. Before the opening face-off of the second game, two days later, the Red Wings were chanting, "Win this one for Gordie." Howe was still in very serious condition. The Maple Leafs were bracing themselves for a Detroit attempt to "get Kennedy."

The game began calmly enough, with only two penalties called in the first period, and Detroit ran up a two-goal lead on scores by Red Kelly and Sid Abel. Joe Carveth got another goal for the Wings midway in the second period, and for a few more moments it appeared that rationality would prevail. Then, "somebody pulled an invisible trigger," wrote Jim Vipond of the Toronto *Globe and Mail*, "and mayhem broke loose."

It started when Red Wing Lee Fogolin sent Kennedy rolling with a stick trip. As play halted and referee Keeling thumbed Fogolin to the penalty box, Ted Lindsay rushed up and cross-checked Kennedy back to the ice. Toronto's Gus Mortson flew at Lindsay, and fights broke out all over the rink. About 20 feet out from the Detroit goal Toronto defenseman Jim Thomson fell, and Detroit's Leo Reise bludgeoned him across the head and shoulders with his stick. Then Reise spotted Kennedy and went over to get in some more stickwork, this time across Kennedy's shoulders.

Lindsay rushed at Kennedy again, his stick held high; then Abel came on, flailing with his fists. A fan grabbed Kennedy and held his arms as other Wings struck him. Toronto goalie Turk Broda, handicapped by 35 pounds of leg pads, trundled over to assist his teammate, but Abel and Lindsay persisted in their determined efforts.

When the fighting finally subsided, the penalties

were sorted out, the ice was cleared of debris, and the game was resumed. Detroit was the ultimate victor. The Wings trooped happily into their dressing room with Lindsay marching proudly at their head shouting for all the world to hear: "We won for Gordie!"

Kennedy emerged from the fracas with a black eye and a cut above his lip. All he would say was, "The game's over. They won it."

Everyone agreed that something must be done to stop the fighting. President Campbell responded with a loud gavel, warning that "very substantial fines and suspensions" would be applied if necessary to stop bitter feuding between the Maple Leafs and the Red Wings. He ordered the standby referee to act as a linesman in future games and ordered the managers and coaches of both teams to a meeting to settle "any possible misunderstandings . . . of what is being done."

"Hockey is a tough and rugged game at the best of times," said Campbell, "but the stick-swinging which took place has no place in the game at any time."

Referee Bill Chadwick tolerated no nonsense in the third game, which was played at Maple Leaf Gardens in Toronto. He whistled Howie Meeker off the ice in the opening minute, after which he had to penalize only two other players. Equilibrium seemed to have been restored, and both teams were playing hockey according to the book. The Leafs scored twice in the second period, on goals by Joe Klukay and Max

Bentley, and they won the game 2–0, to take a lead of two games to one in the series.

Detroit tied the series with a 2–1 victory in the fourth game; then the Leafs went ahead again, blanking the Wings 2–0. Though Howe was lost to them for the playoffs, the Red Wings defeated the Leafs 4–0 at Toronto in the sixth game, carrying the semifinal series to a seventh and deciding game at Detroit.

In the final game the teams battled through three periods of regulation time without a goal. Checking remained close through the opening eight minutes of the sudden-death overtime. Then Detroit's Leo Reise, the man who had been involved in the stick-swinging in the second game, broke through to score the winning goal in the ninth minute of play. The Detroit fans were delirious. After five straight playoff eliminations at the hands of the Maple Leafs, the Red Wings had finally won—even without the scoring of Gordie Howe.

Ted Lindsay summed up the victory: "The injury to Gordie set off the explosion within us. We blew our tops a bit, but believe me, when there's so much at stake out there, you sometimes get out of control."

The Red Wings went on to win the Stanley Cup in the finals from the New York Rangers in seven hard-fought games. But the Kennedy feud didn't simmer down. Detroiters remained convinced that Teeder had savagely butt-ended or had done something viciously illegal to Howe. Although Gordie returned for the 1950–51 season seemingly a new and healthy man, the Wings went after Kennedy whenever possible.

"They rode Kennedy unmercifully from the bench," said Munson Campbell, an NHL executive who then was a frequent visitor to the Red Wings' dressing room. "Once, the Detroit club came to Toronto around Christmas time for a game with the Leafs. It so happened that there was a picture in the papers of Kennedy sending a holiday greeting to his mother. Well, that night Lindsay was on the bench needling Kennedy unmercifully, saying, 'Ding-a-ling, Ted, it's Ma on the phone' and things like that. It became a very personal vendetta because Gordie came so close to dying.

"It wasn't just Lindsay who gave Kennedy the business but Ted was so much better at needling and he was so close to Gordie. It became a personal vendetta—a chip, a chop, a high-stick, a butt end here and there—that kept eroding at Kennedy. I think that when it was all over the feud took ten years off Ted Kennedy's life. He [Lindsay] made him pay for it."

But not before the Toronto captain had proven that he had the courage of a lion. The Maple Leafs rebounded in the spring of 1951 and regained the Stanley Cup with Captain Teeder leading the way.

That, however, was to be the Maple Leafs' last gasp for many years to come. Toronto was in decline, and the new powerhouse—winner of the regular-season title year after year—was Detroit. The Red Wings got

Bruised and battered, Maple Leaf star Teeder Kennedy rests after a game.

the last laugh in the semifinal round of the 1952 Stanley Cup playoffs.

The series opened in Detroit with the Red Wings easy winners, 3–0. "Don't worry, fellows," said captain Kennedy, "only four more games against these guys and we'll have them." It was a hollow promise. The Red Wings seemed stronger than ever, especially on defense. In the second game they scored a goal in the first period and held the Leafs scoreless. The Maple Leafs returned to Toronto down two games to none.

They couldn't stop Detroit's mighty machine even in Maple Leaf Gardens. When the final buzzer sounded in the third game the score was 6–2 for Detroit.

"In simple language," wrote Al Nickleson in the Toronto *Globe and Mail*, "the defending champions had a lesson in how to play hockey thrown at them by possibly the greatest Detroit team in a long line of standout clubs."

The Red Wings were awesome, to be sure, but the Maple Leafs could do nothing right any more. "The puck rolls when it should slide," said Toronto's Max Bentley. "It hops over your stick instead of onto it. We shoot and it hits a leg and deflects away. They shoot, and it hits a leg and goes in. Other years we played Detroit we got those breaks. This year they're getting them."

But the series wasn't over. In an effort to restore their faith in the Maple Leafs, diehard Toronto fans recalled the gallant 1942 comeback. Surely the Leafs would not be beaten in four straight games.

Toronto went ahead 1–0 in the fourth game at 2:56 of the first period, and the hopes of 13,574 fans in Maple Leaf Gardens soared. "The Leafs came out like the fighting, hard-hitting Toronto teams of old," said Al Nickleson. "They battled fiercest when the odds were greatest."

It was unfortunately too little and too late. Ted Lindsay tied the game for Detroit, and Tony Leswick put the Red Wings ahead to stay before the first period had ended. From that point on Toronto played a desperate and heart-breaking game of catch-up and never could haul down the sensational Red Wings machine. Sid Abel scored for Detroit in the second period, and the game ended with Detroit on top 3–1. The mighty Red Wings then went on to rout the Montreal Canadiens in four straight games to take the Stanley Cup.

Although some bitterness remained between the clubs for years after, the rivalry was over for years to come. Toronto sank in the standings, and in 1956 Teeder Kennedy retired—seemingly old before his time. Ted Lindsay—Kennedy's most outspoken antagonist—played nearly a decade longer, hanging up his skates in 1965. Most amazing of all, Gordie Howe, whose injury had brought the bitter rivalry to a boil, played for Detroit until 1971. And in 1974 he nearly led the World Hockey Association in scoring at the age of 46. One of his linemates was his son, Mark, who had not even been born when Gordie crashed into the boards, nearly ending his career 24 years too soon.

Rocket Richard vs. Gordie Howe

They both played right wing. Both were formidably built with enormous strength in the arms and legs. Both were superior skaters, rough players and great shooters.

Yet as individuals and performers, Maurice "the Rocket" Richard and Gordie Howe were as different as night and day.

A French-Canadian with fierce-looking eyes and glistening black hair, the Rocket was Montreal's gift to hockey and the hero of Quebec province. When Richard skated for the Canadiens he always seemed on the brink of an explosion, either with his stick or his fists.

By contrast, Howe grew up in the wide-open spaces of English-speaking Saskatchewan in the Canadian West. Unlike Richard, who spoke little English, Howe had a Western drawl that symbolized his relaxed approach to life in general and hockey in particular.

There were several reasons why the Richard-Howe rivalry developed to such a high pitch of intensity

Montreal's fierce Rocket Richard carries the puck down the ice.

during the late 1940s and early '50s. Perhaps most important was the fact that their respective teams, the Detroit Red Wings and Montreal Canadiens, had a long history of hostility. Howe and Richard merely fed the fires of fury between the clubs.

Then there was the ethnic question. Richard symbolized the French-Canadian minority in Canada. When The Rocket scored against an English-speaking team all of Quebec rejoiced. He was to French-Canada what Joe Louis had been to America's black population in the 1930s and '40s. Howe, of course, represented the English Canadians who were less intense but no less serious about their hockey.

But most important, Howe and Richard were the best in their business. Richard entered the league in 1942 at the age of 21 after an illustrious career in amateur hockey. Howe, seven years younger, came to the Detroit Red Wings in 1946 when he was only 18. Within five years, no one doubted that Richard and Howe were the two greatest players in hockey. The only question was which one was better. The argument was still raging 25 years later.

Richard got a big head start. In 1944–45 he took his first giant step toward ice immortality when he scored 50 goals in 50 games, an astonishing accomplishment, and also added 23 assists for a total of 73 points. In 1945–46, the year young Gordie Howe turned pro with the Omaha Knights, Richard was already the biggest name in the National Hockey League. He played on the famous Punch Line with Toe Blake and Elmer

Lach, but he put his linemates into the shade.

Richard's style of play was explosive, aggressive and at all times colorful. His flair for the dramatic reminded fans of Babe Ruth. And like Ruth, Richard was first and foremost a scorer. Probably no player in the history of professional hockey was as fearsome as Richard inside the enemy's blue line.

In Montreal, for example, they still talk about what is referred to simply as "the Boston goal." Richard scored it late in the third period of a Stanley Cup playoff game against Boston in 1952. The Bruins had just completed a rush on the Canadien goal. Richard retrieved the disk in front of the Montreal net and started up-ice. He swerved around a Boston wingman who was trying to check him, cut to the right boards at the red line and headed toward Bruin ice.

At the Boston line Richard fended off a Bruin defenseman with his left arm, but still was steered into the corner to the right of the Boston net. It appeared that the puck would be frozen there. But somehow, Richard managed to break free from the defenseman. With a swoop of his stick he recovered the puck and skated laterally toward the Boston goal. With a quick feint, Richard brought the goaltender to his knees. Then he fired into the upper right-hand corner of the net. Richard's score broke a 1–1 tie and gave Montreal the game.

In scoring territory then, Richard was a furious and feverish hockey player, completely obsessed with scoring. "When he came flying in toward you with the puck on his stick," goalie Glenn Hall once said, "Richard's eyes were all lit up, flashing and gleaming like a pinball machine."

Richard, however, had relatively little use for the other aspects of the game. His defensive play was often loose, sometimes downright sloppy. He never was much of a checker. Nor was he overly concerned with the assist column of the scoring sheet. Given the option of shooting or passing to a teammate with better position, Richard would shoot. Although he led the league in goals scored five times, he never led in scoring points (goals plus assists). But then few ever thought to complain that Babe Ruth hit too few singles—and few Montreal fans complained about the Rocket.

But the Rocket was not a selfish scorer. In fact, his most striking characteristic was a fierce desire to win games for the Canadiens. In one game against the Red Wings, Detroit manager Jack Adams sent Ted Lindsay out to harass Richard. The Rocket retaliated and wound up with a five-minute major penalty. While he stewed in the penalty box, Detroit rapidly scored two goals. "Perturbed by the turn of events," said author Vince Lunny, "rivers of anger scalded the Rocket's brain. When he served his time he leaped from the bench like all hell breaking loose."

The Rocket pounced on the puck and drove it past the Detroit goaltender. He remained on the ice and seconds later took a pass from Lach, eluded the defense, and fired one of his patented backhanders into the twine. By now coach Irvin figured the Rocket was ready for a rest and called him to the bench. "Never mind," countered Richard, "I had my rest in the penalty box."

Lach won the next face-off and passed the puck to a teammate who relayed it to Richard. He skated straight into Lindsay, bowling him over, and scored again. The Canadiens won 3–2.

Author Lunny had great insight into the Rocket. "His nerves are as taut as trout lines," he wrote. "If he had to keep the tension bottled up within himself, he'd probably blow up. Luckily, hockey is a physical contact sport which provides a release for the nervous tension that twists his stomach into knots and threatens a mental breakdown."

Around the rink he rarely betrayed a smile. Once after a game with the Maple Leafs in which he scored a three-goal hat trick, Toronto photographer Nat Turofsky asked him to smile for the camera.

"What have I to smile about?" asked Richard. "We only tied tonight."

Like the good photographer he was, Turofsky persisted. "C'mon, Rocket," he urged, "smile and kiss the stick!"

"Kiss it yourself," snapped Richard. And that was that!

In the 1950–51 season, Richard was fulfilling all the rave notices that suggested he was hockey's greatest goal-scorer. "He can shoot from any angle," said goalie Frank Brimsek. "You play him for a shot to the upper

corner and the Rocket wheels around and fires a backhander into the near, lower part of the net."

"When Richard breaks on one defenseman," said Boston's Murray Henderson, "there's no telling what he'll do. If he gets his body between you and the puck, you just can't get at it. He cradles the puck on the

The Rocket scores against Toronto goalie Harry Lumley in 1953.

blade of his stick, steers it with one hand, and wards off his check with the other. Strong? That guy is like an ox, but he sure doesn't look it."

But success did not soften the Rocket, especially since he was being mauled by the frustrated opposition. In March 1951 he was thrown into a goal post by

Detroit's Sid Abel and drew first a 10-minute major penalty, then a match penalty and a fine for his complaints to referee Hugh McLean and fights with Red Wing Leo Reise and lineman Joe Primeau.

The following night he saw referee McLean in a New York hotel lobby and according to observers, he might have beaten the referee up if two Canadien staff members had not restrained him. League president Clarence Campbell fined Richard $500 for the outburst, and newspapers in enemy towns claimed the Rocket should have been suspended.

But Richard continued to shine on the ice. In the first round of the 1951 playoffs the Canadiens faced the powerful Red Wings, led by Gordie Howe, who was challenging the Rocket for the title of best player in hockey. The opening game in Detroit was tied 2–2 after regulation time. In the first period of overtime neither team scored. Another twenty minutes were played and still no decision. Unbelievably, it was past midnight when the third sudden death was completed and the score remained the same. By now the leg-weary athletes were having trouble racing up and down the ice, and it appeared that the game would last until morning without a score.

Montreal coach Dick Irvin sent his bread-and-butter scorer, the Rocket, onto the ice for the start of the fourth overtime and a minute went by without any decisive thrust. It was almost 1:10 A.M. when the Red Wing defense attempted to launch an attack. Richard saw the pass coming and pounced on the puck like a leopard. "He sped past the Detroit defense," said the Canadian Press, "with a blazing burst of speed. Alone in front of the net, he paused, then lined a ten-footer past Terry Sawchuk."

Amazingly, the second game of the series, also at Detroit's Olympia Stadium, was a virtual duplicate of the first. The teams were tied this time 0–0, at the end of regulation time. They struggled without success through two scoreless sudden-death periods and were on the brink of collapse. Then at 2:10 of the third overtime Montreal defenseman Bud MacPherson commanded the puck and delivered a crisp pass to Billy Reay near the Detroit goal. Reay tempted Sawchuk with a feint, then skimmed the puck to Richard who was zooming in from the left. Richard's shot was so hard it nearly tore a hole in the mesh, and the Canadiens were now ahead two games to none.

"He is as great an opportunist as the game has ever known," said Baz O'Meara in the Montreal *Star*. "His great adversary, Gordie Howe, was a spent force. Richard may be the most unpredictable, temperamental cuss that ever laced on a skate, but he is the special delivery kid."

Detroit rebounded to win the next two games in Montreal but it was the Rocket again in the fifth game, scoring the winning goal in the third period as the Canadiens prevailed, 5–2.

The sixth game of the series was described by Toronto's King Clancy as "the greatest game I ever saw in my life." Montreal went ahead on a shot by

Reay in the first period. The Red Wings tied it less than a minute later. Then the Rocket and then Ken Mosdell each beat Sawchuk to put the contest out of Detroit's reach. Montreal finished on top, 3–2, winning the Stanley Cup. When it was over the Rocket was unpredictable as ever. "He was the quietest of the winners," observed Montreal writer Vic Morris, Jr. "He changed his uniform without saying a word."

Richard had out-performed and outscored Howe in those playoffs. But it was beginning to be clear that the future would belong to the Detroit star. In 1951 he was still only 23 years old (Richard was 30), and he had won the scoring championship for the first time.

Gordie had made his NHL debut with the Detroit Red Wings in 1946. The smooth-skating kid from Floral, Saskatchewan, hardly drew a nod from Richard that first season. And why should he have? Howe scored only seven goals in 58 games and became better known for his fighting ability than his offensive powers.

"Don't worry about Gordie," said Red Wing manager Jack Adams. "He needs another year or two; then he'll be one of the best around, and that includes the Rocket."

Adams was right. Howe improved with each year, especially after he was placed on a line with hard-nosed center Sid Abel and a smallish but tough left wing named Ted Lindsay. They were appropriately named "The Production Line" and proved their right to the title by finishing one-two-three in scoring during the 1949–50 season.

Young Gordie Howe, Richard's biggest challenger.

In the first game of the 1950 playoffs Howe suffered an injury that threatened his life and his hockey career. He fell into the boards, fracturing his skull, and was in critical condition for days. But by the time the 1950–51 season got underway he was back. The injury had given him a strange tic—he seemed to be blinking his eyes continually—but his hockey skills seemed unaffected.

The Montreal fans, who idolized their Rocket, recognized Gordie's promise. Each time Howe skated on Montreal ice he was assailed with boos because he had become a threat to Richard's dominance. In one game at the Canadiens' Forum, Gordie reached a milestone. On February 17, 1951, against goalie Gerry MacNeil, he scored his 100th goal. Most embarrassing of all, it was "Rocket Richard Night."

That 100th goal was an omen of things to come. For at the end of the season Howe displaced Richard at right wing on the first team of All-Stars. More than that, Howe was fast displacing Richard as the most celebrated player in professional hockey. Howe kept his First All-Star spot for four seasons in a row.

Howe's rise to the "superstar" class coincided with the start of a four-year period during which the Red Wings overshadowed the Canadiens. Beginning with the 1951–52 campaign and continuing through the 1954–55 season, Detroit finished atop the league, while Montreal placed second. During that same period, the Wings won three Stanley Cup championships, and the

Canadiens took the Cup but once.

Howe regarded the 1951–52 team as the best Detroit club he played on. And with good reason. That season Detroit compiled 100 points in 70 games—while second-place Montreal picked up only 78. In the first round of the Stanley Cup playoffs, the Wings beat Toronto four straight. In the final round against Richard's Canadiens, the Wings again won four straight.

"The way we were playing," Howe said in talking about the Stanley Cup sweep, "I think we could have won 35 straight."

Howe appeared so strong on the ice that one suspected he could score at his pleasure. For instance, he demoralized the Maple Leafs in the third game of the Stanley Cup semifinal round in Toronto on March 29, 1952, shooting with bomb-sight accuracy and brushing past enemy defenders as if they were made of cardboard.

When Gordie was at the top of his game, as he was that night, he skittered effortlessly from one end of the rink to another, like a water bug on a pond. His shot had a deceptive quality about it. Instead of being heralded with a flamboyant wind-up—as was Bobby Hull's slapshot—Howe's blast was like a gun with a silencer over its muzzle. His shot was unobtrusive, but accurate and tremendously powerful.

Unlike Rocket Richard, Howe occasionally would return to his boyhood traits and just plain fool around

with his ability—and his opponents. In that memorable Toronto game—which Detroit won 6–2—Howe broke away from the entire Leaf team at center ice and cruised in on rotund Turk Broda, helplessly alone in front of the Leaf net.

Almost dreamily, Gordie loped along the left side, nonchalantly executed a couple of feints that lured Broda several feet out of the net and then, with nothing but the six feet of yawning cage in front of him, Howe playfully shot for the far right post, trying for a billiard carom shot. This was the only challenge left for him. The puck nicked the right post and slipped harmlessly into the corner.

Howe worry? Why should he? Next time he wouldn't fool around, and the puck would go in.

That year, Howe scored 47 goals in regular-season play and added 39 assists to lead the league in total points and goals. He also was awarded the Hart Trophy as the league's most valuable player.

Laconic to the point of seeming not to care, Howe never was nearly as good copy to newsmen as Richard. Gordie's prairie wit always was good for laughs now and then but he usually maintained a low profile and avoided controversy whenever possible. If awards were given for drama, Howe would not have had a chance.

In 1954–55 the Red Wings won the Stanley Cup again, but when the votes were in for the All-Star team, Rocket Richard had gotten back his place on the First Team. Then in 1955–56 the Rocket led the Canadiens back to the Stanley Cup.

Eyes on the puck, Howe (9) gets set to race down the ice.

Maturity had made him a new man. Explosions were rare, yet the goals still came. He was surrounded by a star-studded line-up which included Doug Harvey, Dickie Moore, Jacques Plante, Bernie Geoffrion, Jean Beliveau and Tom Johnson. And they made life a lot easier for Richard, who frequently believed that he single-handedly had to carry the Canadiens on his broad shoulders.

The Rocket appeared more relaxed than ever and he became almost beloved in arenas throughout the league. When he scored a three-goal hat trick at Olympia Stadium in Detroit in October 1957, Richard received a standing ovation. "It took sixteen years," said Detroit writer Marshall Dann, "but the time finally came when Rocket Richard drew more cheers than jeers in Detroit." Soon after, the Rocket soon scored his 500th NHL goal.

Richard had leaped ahead of the scoring race in 1957–58 like a Kentucky Derby sprinter. By the second week in November it appeared that, at last, he would go on to win that elusive scoring championship. Then tragedy struck. While playing against the Maple Leafs at Toronto on November 13, the Rocket tangled with defenseman Marc Reaume of the Leafs. It was an innocent collision, ironically different from so many of Richard's clashes with his foes.

As Reaume scrambled to his feet, his razor-sharp skate sliced between Richard's tendon guard and his stocking, almost cutting Richard's tendon in half. The Rocket was carried into Maple Leaf Gardens' hospital

Richard accepts congratulations after the Canadiens' 1958 Stanley Cup victory.

where Dr. Jim Murray administered fifteen stitches to the wound. "He was lucky," said Dr. Murray. "Just a shade more and the tendon would have snapped. Had this happened it could very well have meant the end of his career."

Richard was thirty-six years old at the time of the mishap and it was freely predicted that this would be the end of the line for him, whether he recovered or not. But by February 20, 1958, scarcely three months later, Richard was back in the line-up and celebrated his return with two goals and two near-misses.

The Rocket began to realize that he could no longer maintain his breathtaking pace as a regular, yet he was reluctant to quit. And why should he? Certainly, Richard was not hurting the Canadiens. While Howe's Red Wings were starving for another Stanley Cup win, Richard's Flying Frenchmen were winning the coveted trophy an unprecedented five consecutive seasons from 1956 through 1960.

In the fall of 1960, the Rocket knew that he could not continue. On September 15, 1960, he called it quits. After 978 regular season games and 133 playoff matches, Richard retired. He had scored 544 goals in regular season play and 82 more in the playoffs—far more than any player in hockey history. He left the field to Gordie Howe, and from 1960 on, Gordie competed not against the Rocket himself but against the memory of hockey's most spectacular scorer.

As the years passed, Howe proved again and again

that he was the greatest all-round player. He was an outstanding checker and defensive player. He worked equally as well as a penalty-killer and as the key man in the Detroit power play. In other words, he excelled in all phases of the game.

Certainly, Howe loved to score. But he didn't try to carry the whole load himself. His unselfishness always amazed his fans and his teammates. In the last game of the 1959–60 season, for example, Detroit rookie Murray Oliver needed one goal to collect a cash bonus for netting 20 goals in his first season. Midway through the game Howe told Oliver:"The next time we're on ice, get in front of the net." Oliver followed instructions. Howe carried to the blue line, shot, and Oliver tipped the puck in for the score.

Then, in an uncharacteristic burst of bravado, Howe skated to the Detroit bench and called out, "Anyone else need any bonus money?"

A few seasons later, Howe was working under a bonus set-up that paid a bonus for any goals he scored over 35. In a game against Boston, Howe was credited with the first goal of the night. He skated over to the official scorer and asked for a correction, explaining that Parker MacDonald was entitled to the goal. In the second period the Wings scored again. Again Howe received credit for the goal. Again he disagreed with the official scorer and the goal was credited to Alex Delvecchio. He stood to make money, but he refused to take credit for others' accomplishments.

As intense and tough as ever, Gordie Howe takes the ice with his son Mark (left) for the Houston Aeros in 1973–74.

On the negative side, Howe also became a legend for his rough—some said dirty—play. "He was a dirty hockey player," said Richard. "And he would take absolutely nothing from anybody. If you gave him a bad check, you could be sure that he'd get even with you—in spades! But he wouldn't start it."

Enemy defenders learned to give Gordie plenty of room to maneuver because if they crowded him too often they might find a hockey stick down their throats. Gordie's defenders claimed that a super-scorer had to defend himself or he would be the victim of every illegal defensive move in the book.

As the 1960s ended, Howe was past 40, but he was still playing regularly and well. Amazed hockey experts said that if Howe never won anything else, he should get the prize as the game's most durable player. But Gordie didn't have to rely on newly created awards. He had scored more than 700 goals, more than Richard had ever dreamed of. He had been an All-Star for so many seasons people wondered what the team would do without him. And he had been chosen the league's most valuable player six times.

At the end of the 1970–71 season, Howe retired and took an administrative job with the Red Wings. But that was still not the end of his career. In 1973 he signed to play with the Houston Aeros of the new World Hockey Association. In his first season, he nearly led the league in scoring. At 46 years old, Howe was still adding to his enormous record as a superstar over three hockey generations.

Rocket Richard had the last word on Gordie Howe: "Looking back, I would say that Howe is the best all-round hockey player I've ever seen, and that includes Bobby Hull and Bobby Orr. I have to say that it was an honor to play against Gordie Howe and be compared to him."

Philadelphia Flyers
vs.
St. Louis Blues

From the very beginning in 1967, the Philadelphia Flyers and St. Louis Blues did not like each other. And as season followed season the relationship grew progressively worse. The two teams, which would seemingly stop at nothing to beat the other, provided the first great rivalry between the new teams in the National Hockey League.

Both the Flyers and Blues were charter members of the NHL's grand expansion operation in 1967–68. In the first season of play Philadelphia had the better players and finished first in the West Division (which then was made up of six new teams). But while Philadelphia won the games, St. Louis won the fights. The Flyers put the accent on artistry in that opening year while the Blues searched for musclemen. The St. Louis defense was built around Bob and Barclay Plager, brothers who would rather fight than score. They were helped by Noel Picard, a Bunyanesque defenseman who once had been a bouncer in a

Canadian bar. By contrast, the Flyer defense looked like the Seven Dwarfs.

Skirmishing between the teams began during the regular 1967–68 season. The Flyers enjoyed a brilliant homestretch run to nail down their pennant in the West Division. They beat St. Louis 2–0 late in March to virtually eliminate the Blues from playoff contention. But the Blues rallied and finished third, gaining the right to meet Philadelphia in the opening round of the playoffs for the Stanley Cup.

The Flyers, of course, were favored to win the best-of-seven series. Since they had finished first in their division, they would have the advantage of home ice if the series went the full seven games. However, the Philadelphians' confidence was shattered in the opening game on April 4, 1968.

Playing the puck as well as they played the man, St. Louis dominated the home club and kept them off the score sheet. One of the Blues' less conspicuous belters, Jim Roberts, scored the one and only goal of the game.

The Flyers quickly retaliated in the second game, winning 4–3 on Leon Rochefort's goal, but they received a fierce pounding from the Blues' big guns. The pattern of the series had been established: if the Flyers could withstand the Blues' muscle, they might prevail. If not, St. Louis would win the round.

Playing at their home arena, St. Louis took the series lead in the third game. Forward Larry Keenan scored in the second sudden-death overtime for a 3–2 tri-

The Blues' Gary Sabourin and the Flyers' Ed Van Impe tangle in a 1970 game.

umph. They followed that up by routing the Flyers 5–2 on April 11. With an advantage of three games to one, they appeared ready to move ahead to the next playoff round.

But when the teams returned to the Spectrum in Philadelphia for the fifth game, a new level of savagery was achieved for expansion hockey. Patsies no more, the Flyers traded blow for blow with the Blues. Then at 9:13 of the third period all hell broke loose.

The Blues' Picard and Flyer Claude Laforge started the brawl and soon both benches emptied and punches were being thrown all over the ice. The Flyers didn't win all the fights but the fact remained that they did fight. Picard knocked the smaller Laforge to the ice bleeding from the mouth. The Flyers' forward limped to the dressing room where 14 stitches were required to close his wound. But by this time the Flyers had won the game. They were still down three games to two, but their new tough tactics had kept them in the running.

Afterward charges flew back and forth from the enemy camps like artillery shells across no-man's-land. "That guy Picard hit Laforge from behind," snapped Flyer manager Bud Poile. "That doesn't take much guts."

NHL President Clarence Campbell, who already had leveled $3,800 in fines against battlers from the two teams, stepped into the mediator's position. After reviewing the evidence, Campbell blamed St. Louis coach Scotty Bowman and Philadelphia coach Keith Allen for inspiring the endless brawling. "They have failed completely to maintain discipline and control over the players so often that their failure is inexcusable," he said.

Barclay Plager (8) tries to get in to help Noel Picard (lost in crowd) as the Blues tangle with the Vancouver Canucks in 1970.

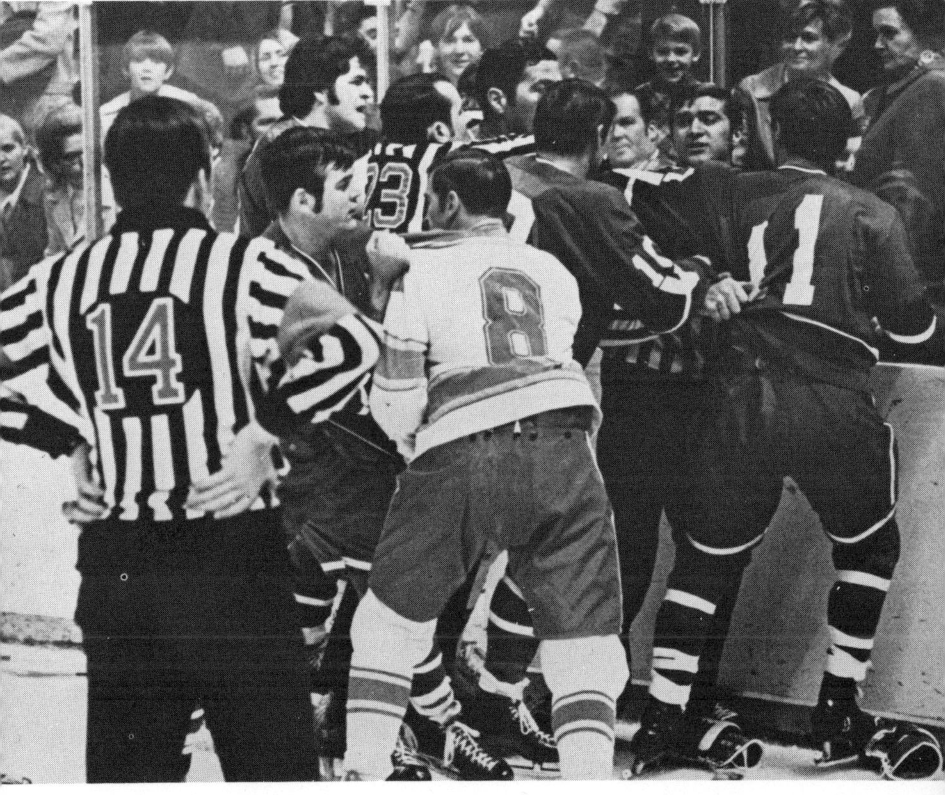

The inspired Flyers returned to St. Louis where they tied the series at three games apiece and set the stage for the seventh and final contest on April 18, 1968, at Philadelphia's Spectrum.

By now the clubs had expended so much energy on fighting they were compelled to concentrate on defense and scoring. What resulted was a minor classic. The score was tied 1–1 in the second period when veteran St. Louis defenseman Doug Harvey skimmed a perfect pass to Keenan, an earlier hero for the Blues. The young forward galloped over the blue line and beat goalie Bernie Parent for what proved to be the winning goal. Red Berenson scored an insurance goal into an open net in the final minute of play as St. Louis won the game 3–1 and went on to the semifinal round of the playoffs.

The victory had long-range significance for the two teams. It indicated that the Blues' intimidating tactics could work, and allowed St. Louis to gain a vital psychological edge over their Pennsylvania rivals.

In 1968–69 the Flyers were deposed by the very same Blues as regular-season champs. St. Louis clinched first place on March 8, 1969, and the Flyers finished a distant third. But once again the two teams met in the opening playoff round, so the Flyers had a quick chance for revenge.

This time the series was no contest. Hitting harder than in 1968, the Blues sent Flyer forwards scattering off in all directions when they tried to get the puck. St.

Louis won the first two games at home.

Frustrated to the core, Spectrum fans attempted to take up where their non-fighting Flyers had left off. In the third game, at Philadelphia's Spectrum, Flyers fans continuously challenged coach Scotty Bowman and his visitors.

"When the Blues strode to the ice," said Chuck Newman of the Philadelphia *Inquirer*, "they were pelted verbally and with debris from the fans above."

Attempts by NHL Supervisor of Officials Frank Udvari to obtain calm went for naught. Flyer president Ed Snider did his best to rationalize the acts of anti-Blues harassment. "It's just that St. Louis is our blood rival," said Snider. "The game is just so emotional it brings on these things."

Throwing coins onto the ice is one of the most dangerous things hockey fans can do. They imbed themselves in the ice and then trip up a speeding skater, threatening serious injury. Blues defenseman Bob Plager wryly noted that the Flyers fans even did a bad job of that. "When they throw coins on the ice they're only pennies," he said. "At least our fans in St. Louis throw nickels."

The harassment ended relatively soon because the Blues won the series in four consecutive games. A year earlier the Flyers had hoped to be the best expansion team in hockey. Now they had lost first place in the West Division and been humiliated two years in a row by the tough St. Louis club. "It bothered me that we

The Flyers began their own roughhouse campaign with players like "Mad Dog" Kelly, who is shown grabbing an opponent by the hair.

were being outhit," said Flyer president Snider. "I knew we had to do something about it."

The "something," of course, was to trade for musclemen who could match the Plagers and Picard punch for punch, if not check for check. "The Flyers' management," wrote Toronto *Star* sports editor Jim Proudfoot, "set out deliberately to assemble a gang of ruffians who would intimidate the opposition that couldn't be defeated in customary ways."

This could not be accomplished overnight. But the Flyers scouts knew what they were after and in 1970 Philadelphia drafted Bob "Mad Dog" Kelly, a 5-foot-10, 190-pound left-winger and signed him to an NHL contract. "Kelly," wrote Proudfoot, "is the pugnacious-type player, more noted for the fights he's instigated and won than for the picturesque goals he's scored."

Kelly scored only 14 goals in 76 NHL games for Philadelphia in the 1970–71 campaign but he clearly showed a desire to battle anyone, anytime. "I know they pay me to hit," Kelly explained. "I like to dig the pucks out and hit people in the process."

Kelly soon would be supported by other sluggers. St. Louis had kept the advantage over the Flyers, but by 1971–72 the Philadelphians had just about pulled even. Whatever edge the Flyers still lacked was made up for by energetic Flyer fans who always seemed to be anxious to personally engage the enemy.

On the night of January 6, 1972, for example, a group of Philadelphia fans instigated what the Philadelphia *Daily News* described as "the biggest brawl in the Flyers' five-year history." Needless to say, the Blues were visiting that night.

In the first period of the match Flyer defenseman Bill Brossart was high-sticked by the Blues' Gary Sabourin. Philadelphia goalie Doug Favell skated to center ice in pursuit of Sabourin. Favell was restrained, but minutes later he skated over to the St. Louis bench and exchanged taunts with the Blues.

A tenuous calm prevalied until Blues coach Al Arbour protested a face-off to referee John Ashley. The official promptly whistled a two-minute "bench" penalty against Arbour.

The Blues' leader exploded and chased after the referee, who headed for the exit that leads to the officials' dressing room. Several St. Louis players congregated near the exit. As Arbour followed Ashley down the runway, according to Arbour, "someone poured beer on me and someone else hit me."

The first stage of a riot had taken place. "All of a sudden," Arbour explained, "everyone was pushing and shoving and I fell on a policeman. Then, I got hit over the head with a billy club."

That was only one of several main-eventers which were exploding at the same time. Fans, who had started the fight by hurling beer and debris at the Blues, soon found themselves under siege as St. Louis players, skates and all, charged up into the grandstands wielding their sticks like bayonets. Among the leaders were Bob Plager, Phil Roberto, John Arbour (no relation to the coach) and Floyd Thomson.

Arbour (the player) claimed he was struck with a hockey stick by police. He later required 40 stitches to close a head wound. Meanwhile, an alarm went out for additional police reinforcements until a total of 150 were summoned to break up the confrontations.

Police said that when they attempted to herd the Blues to their dressing room the hockey players attacked them. However, the St. Louis club president, Sidney Salomon, Jr., accused the Philadelphia police. "That was the worst case of police brutality I've ever seen or heard about," said Salomon. "It was worse than the Chicago riot at the 1968 Democratic convention."

The Flyers' management viewed the riot from a different perspective. They asserted that St. Louis players had no business charging into the audience, carrying 55-inch wooden weapons at the ready. "Using the sticks was horrible," said Flyer boss Ed Snider. "I can understand if the players went to Arbour's aid when he was in trouble, but there was no call for the players to go up into the stands."

Several fans were wounded in the battle, suffering assorted cuts and breaks. When the battle was approaching its peak, a newsman who had just arrived on the scene asked one policeman what was happening.

"It's the St. Louis Blues against the cops," he replied, "and we're winning!"

Police managed to get the players out of the stands

after the initial fight. But then "verbal abuses were exchanged between the fans and players and the players headed back to the stands," according to the police report. "A Sergeant warned them that if they didn't get back on the ice they would all be arrested. At that point the coach [Arbour] said, 'You're not going to lock me up.' He came at the Sergeant and pushed him down the ice. The players started to walk over the Sergeant and head for the fans. One of the players held the Sergeant down on the ice as he attempted to get up.

"As more police poured into the area the players started to skate off, and police escorted them to a tunnel which leads to the dressing room. As they did, the players started to swing wildly over the glass partitions at spectators.

"The police finally got all the players in the tunnel but the players started to swing the hockey sticks at police. The police swung back. One of the officers grabbed a player's stick and hit him with it on the head."

Eventually, the officers restored a semblance of order and the game was resumed. But when it was over the two Arbours, Thomson and Roberto were taken to the South Detective Division where they were charged with assaulting police. At 6 the next morning they were freed on $500 bail each.

What mattered more to the 14,536 fans was the irrevocable fact that St. Louis had won the game, 3–2.

As people filed out of the Spectrum, someone asked, "What were the St. Louis players arrested for? Assault?"

"Yeah," was the reply. "Assault on the Flyers."

The defeat was a meaningful one for Philadelphia. The Flyers were to finish out of a playoff berth on the final night of the season. A win or even a tie against the Blues could have put them into the playoffs.

The worm finally turned for Philadelphia's sextet in

St. Louis' Gary Sabourin scores against the Flyers and the Blues keep the upper hand on the scoreboard.

the autumn of 1972. Club president Ed Snider urged his aides to seek out the biggest, toughest, most competent men available to surround the Flyers' promising young Bobby Clarke.

When the players arrived at the training camp that September it was clear that the Flyers' scouts had done their job well. The crop was big and beefy with a large helping of talent thrown in. Heading the beef trust was Dave Schultz, who was described by *Action Sports Hockey* magazine as "the very toughest guy in hockey."

Among Schultz's more notorious accomplices were Bob "Mad Dog" Kelly, Ross Lonsberry and Don Saleski. These Flyers got the nickname "The Broad Street Bullies," and they worked hard to deserve it. They set a record 1,736 penalty minutes during the 1972–73 campaign. And in the process they took on the Blues.

The decisive turnabout occurred on March 25, 1973, at the Spectrum. Philadelphia won the game, 5–2, but more relevant to the 14,000 spectators were two bouts involving St. Louis strongboy Steve Durbano.

The 6-foot-1, 200-pound Durbano, known affectionately as "Son of Godzilla," was first outfought by Dave Schultz. Later in the game as the teams prepared for a face-off near the Flyers' bench, Durbano went looking for more trouble.

"I was skating by," Durbano explained, "and I saw some guys yelling. So, I took my stick and swung it into the area [of the bench]. It happened that I hit the trainer in the face. The Flyers were mad."

To say the least, Durbano had knocked two teeth out of assistant trainer Jim McKenzie's mouth. "Mad Dog" Kelly leapt off the bench and pounded Durbano across the ice until Durbano finally dropped under a flurry of blows.

Blues captain Barclay Plager realized that his teammate was in trouble and signaled the St. Louis bench for help. But no one volunteered.

In bygone days the entire St. Louis bench would have emptied in a mass reprisal against the Philadelphians, but obviously times had changed. After five years of being intimidated by the Blues, the Flyers at last had done some intimidating of their own.

"When no one came to Durbano's aid," said Flyer coach Fred Shero, "it was a low moment for them."

Now it was time for the St. Louis management to worry. They began recruiting reinforcements during the summer of 1973. One of their first acquisitions was J. Bob "Battleship" Kelly (no relation to Philadelphia's Bob "Mad Dog" Kelly). After the 1973–74 season began St. Louis also obtained Glen Sather, who had been a ruffian with the Big Bad Bruins and later the Rangers.

Respected critics saw the handwriting on the wall and it spelled w-a-r. "The Blues," said Toronto *Star* sports editor Jim Proudfoot, "have started a recruitment drive designed to match the Broad Street Mob."

SHER-WOOD
SHERWOOD

Just how far the warfare would go remained to be seen. Many in hockey disliked the continued race for rougher and rougher players. Although they realized that hockey would always be a rough-and-tumble game, they thought that out-and-out warfare like that between the Flyers and the Blues belittled the skill and finesse that should also be part of the game.

Perhaps the situation was best summed up by Bobby Baun, who for years was a bruising defenseman for the Toronto Maple Leafs. "The interesting thing about these battles of the tough guys," said Baun, "is that nobody really comes out a winner. One guy may think he's the toughest around for a while but, sure as shootin', there'll always be another one to come along and knock him for a loop."

By 1974, the worm had turned. The tough Flyers congratulate goalie Bernie Parent after winning an early playoff round.

Team Canada vs. Soviet National Team

The game of hockey was born, nurtured and developed to its highest level in Canada. Although Canada's national game was officially lacrosse, everyone north of the 48th parallel recognized hockey as the *real* Canadian game. Nearly every player who skated in the National Hockey League was Canadian-born, as was every manager, coach and trainer.

It was generally believed, not only in Canada but in Europe and Asia, that hockey belonged to the Canadians and that any Canadian team was better than a similar team from anywhere else.

All of this was emphatically true until the years following World War II. Then something unusual happened. The Russians, who previously had considered soccer their number one sport, became attracted to ice hockey. The Soviet Union was as far north and as cold as Canada. For millions there it was as natural to ice skate as to walk. Since the long, cold winters provided thousands of natural ice skating rinks from

Leningrad to Vladivostok, the shift to hockey was natural and easy.

In the early 1950s, the Russian team was first recognized as a threat on the international hockey scene. It should be noted here that the top Russian players in all sports are considered "amateurs" and compete against other world-class amateurs. It is generally known that they train all year round and have few if any duties except excelling in sport, so in many respects they are the same as professionals in North American sport. By contrast, the top amateurs in Canada often had other full-time jobs and anyway they were usually either too young or not good enough to play professionally in the National Hockey League.

The Soviets made the first splash in 1954. The top Soviet team entered the world (amateur) hockey championships in Stockholm, Sweden, and played so well they reached the finals against a Canadian team comprised of the best non-professionals in North America. Although the Canadian amateurs were hardly of NHL quality, they *were* Canadians and therefore considered capable of beating anybody.

The Russians won 7–2, and the first chip had been delivered against Canada's image of world-wide hockey superiority. But this was only the beginning. Using unique training techniques and developing their own style, the Russians got better and better while the Canadian amateurs remained static. And this was reflected in the results.

By 1962, the Russians, coached by Anatoli Tarasov

and Arkadi Cherneshev, began a rampage of championship victories that was unparalleled in amateur hockey competition. From 1962 through 1972 the Soviets won 12 out of a possible 13 championships in Olympic and World hockey play.

As Canadian hockey critic Jock Carroll pointed out, Canada was left clinging to the idea that its *professional* players were still the best in the world. And even as the 1970s dawned, most hockey experts agreed that NHL players would make short work of the Soviet National team—if they should ever get the chance. The Russians, encouraged by international amateur hockey officials, still refused to meet professional opponents.

But then Soviet coach Tarasov startled the hockey world by revealing that the Russians would, in fact, be willing to play an NHL team. "I wouldn't care if we got beaten 15–0," said Tarasov. "The score won't matter. What will matter is to determine how our hockey players stand up to the best professionals in North America."

The machinery was set in motion to arrange the game, and after considerable haggling, officials of the NHL and the Soviet Ice Hockey Federation arranged for an eight-game series in September 1972. The first four games would be played in Canada and the final set would be played on Russian ice.

"We used to listen to stories about Canadian hockey as if they were fairy tales," said Tarasov. "That the Canadians were invincible, that the skill of the founders of this game was truly fantastic." Now, thought the Canadians, the Russians would have a chance to see for themselves.

The Canadian team was to be composed of National Hockey League stars and coached by Harry Sinden, who had led the Boston Bruins to the 1970 Stanley Cup victory. Sinden faced two obstacles. A new league, the World Hockey Association had been established and had attracted such superstars as Bobby Hull and goalie Gerry Cheevers. The NHL would not allow such renegades to play for Team Canada. Then too, the games would be held before the regular NHL season, and the coaches would have a minimum of training time to get the pro stars into condition and used to one style of play.

Nevertheless, Team Canada displayed an awesome collection of stars: defensemen Brad Park (New York), Bill White (Chicago) and Don Awrey (Boston); hard-shooting forwards Frank Mahovlich and Yvan Cournoyer (Montreal), Bobby Clarke (Philadelphia) and Phil Esposito (Boston); and goalies Ken Dryden (Montreal), Tony Esposito (Chicago) and Ed Johnston (Boston).

North American hockey experts generally agreed that the Russians would be lucky if they weren't blown out of the rink by the third period of the first game. Some said Team Canada would win all eight games and by substantial margins. Coach Sinden reflected the optimism. "We're gearing to win the first game," he said. "We'll think about the second game after we've won the first. But I have complete confidence in the ability of our team to beat *any* combination of hockey players, any time, any place in the world."

The Russians went about their business with extreme thoroughness. They had spent years scouting the NHL teams, filming big-league games and learning the best of the professional game while discarding the worst. They prepared carefully and thoroughly for their four games in Canada.

In the first Canada–USSR game, Phil Esposito (7) is stopped at the goal crease by goalie Vladislav Tretiak, who is sprawled on the ice.

Team Canada, on the other hand, treated the Russians with a casualness bordering on contempt. Scouts were sent to analyze the Russian brand of hockey but they took the most cursory glance at the Soviet sextet. They returned fully confident that Canada would win, reporting that the Russians' most glaring weakness was in the net. Soviet goaltender Vladislav Tretiak was inferior, they said.

The boasts and predictions finally would be put to

the test on September 2, 1972, when the opening face-off would take place in Montreal. By that day all of Canada was in a frenzy, thirsting for the kill, awaiting the big victory of Team Canada, "the best hockey team in the game's history," according to Frank Orr of the Toronto *Star*.

There were 18,818 spectators in the Forum. The national anthems of Canada and Russia blared over the loudspeaker, then the game began. Almost immediately Phil Esposito drilled a shot past goalie Tretiak and soon after Team Canada scored a second goal.

It appeared that the dam had burst on the Soviets and that all the predictions of a grand—and total—Canadian victory would come true. And much quicker than anybody had suspected. Then, Esposito breached the Russian defenses once more and seemed to have a third Canadian goal on his stick. But this time Tretiak was equal to the occasion and blunted the drive.

The myth of Canadian supremacy was about to fall. Instead of retreating in disarray, the Russians regrouped and poured into Canadian territory, testing goalie Ken Dryden again and again. The NHL stars were flabbergasted. Gradually they just fell apart as a team before the astonished eyes of their fans. In no time at all Russia had tied, then soared ahead, and finally put the game completely out of reach of the home team. When the final buzzer sounded, Team Canada had been humiliated by a score of 7–3!

"Seldom since Goliath contemptuously looked at David can an opponent have been so grossly under-

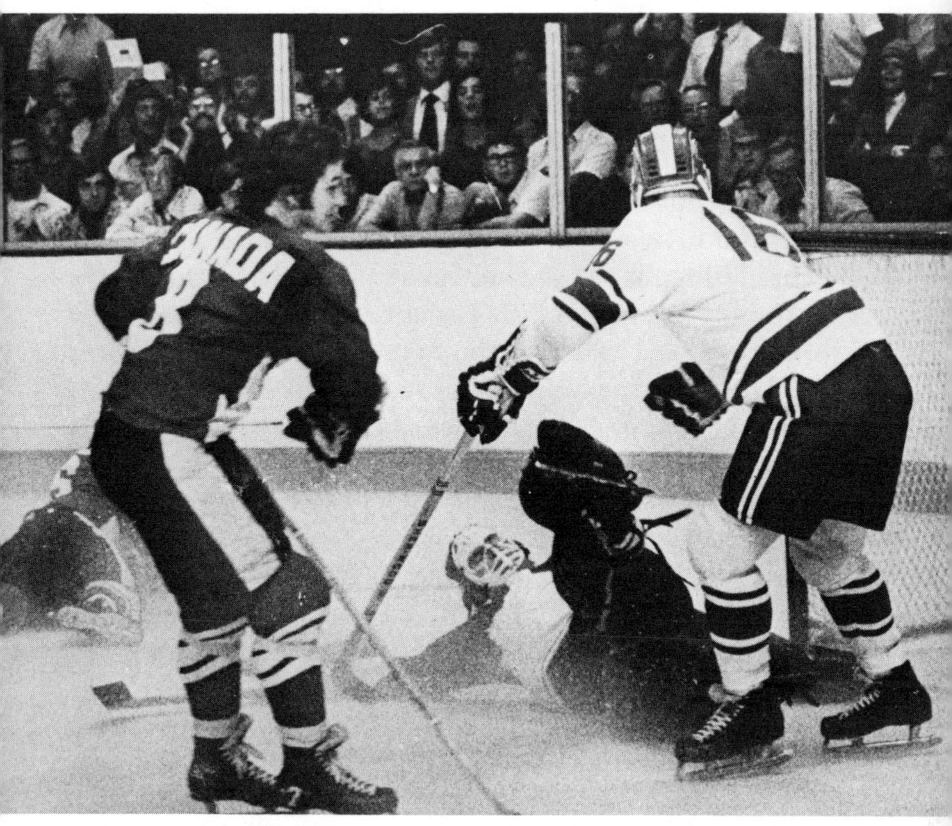

Vladimir Petrov scores against Team Canada goalie Ken Dryden as the Russian team takes an easy victory in game one.

rated as we underrated the Russian Nationals," said an editorial in The Toronto *Star*. "All Canadians concerned shared in this error."

All of a sudden Canadians realized that they no longer reigned supreme in the hockey world. NHL owners paid their compliments to the Russians in the only way they knew—by offering them professional contracts.

"How much do you want for Valery Kharlamov?" Toronto Maple Leafs President Harold Ballard asked Soviet hockey officials. "I'll give you one million dollars and a future draft choice."

The Russians said "thanks, but no thanks" and began preparing for the second game of the series; this one at Maple Leaf Gardens in Toronto. A funereal air covered Canada as a result of the opening game defeat. Some NHL skaters admitted that it was foolish for players and correspondents to have been so overwhelmingly sure of a Team Canada sweep. "I never like going into a series being a favorite," said Boston's Phil Esposito, "no matter where I play."

Team Canada no longer was a favorite but it was not an underdog either. Most experts believed that the second game would be critical in determining the remainder of the series.

The Canadians came through, and fans salvaged a little of their national pride. At Maple Leaf Gardens, Team Canada skated like a team possessed and rumbled to a 4–1 victory over the Soviet National Team.

Chicago Black Hawk goaltender Tony Esposito was splendid in repulsing the skittering Russians, especially in the first period when the visitors threatened to bust the game wide open. And this time the NHL players used their bodies to greater advantage, checking more tenaciously than in a Stanley Cup final game. For a change, coach Sinden was pleased. "We didn't run around like we did in the first game," said Sinden. "We had control in position play."

The impressive performance filled Canadians with new confidence. The loss in the first game now was treated as a freak caused by overconfidence. On to Winnipeg the teams moved for game three.

More than anything, the third game seemed to symbolize the relative merits of both teams. By the end of the second period the score was tied 4–4. The clubs played through the final 20 minutes without another score and the game ended in a 4–4 draw. The result was summed up in a dispatch by Tass, the official Soviet news agency: "The match proved that two really equal, splendid teams were meeting."

This was small consolation to 20,000,000 Canadians who had hoped for an overwhelming victory. There would be one more chance on home ice—in Vancouver. But all was not well with Team Canada. There had been some grumbling even before the series began. The NHL stars had interrupted their vacations to play. They were being paid very little. And there was always the chance they might be injured. After the series started, some top stars didn't get much playing time, and their complaints only made things worse.

More than 18,000 jammed the Pacific Coliseum in Vancouver for game four, expecting the best from Team Canada. Instead they were rewarded with an almost perfect game by the Russians and what frequently appeared to be a disorderly retreat by Team Canada.

Wave after wave of Soviet forwards penetrated the Canadian defenses, pouring five goals past goalie Dryden. Team Canada managed three scores against the acrobatic Tretiak, who was proving to be not inferior at all. The NHL players were subjected to a cascade of boos from their own fans, and after the game several players openly criticized their countrymen for lack of support.

In any event, the Russians now led the series two games to one with one tie as the teams jetted to Moscow for the next four contests. It had become apparent even to the most partisan NHL fan that the Soviet hockey club was as good as, if not better than, the best professionals in North America.

"They play this game," said coach Sinden, "as though there were no scoreboard, no ups and downs. We don't."

Team Canada had several days to reorganize its forces before the series resumed on September 22, 1972, in Moscow. A short exhibition series had been planned for the NHL stickhandlers against Swedish teams as a leisurely tune-up for Moscow, but instead it was another small disaster which further upset members of the Canadian entourage.

Curiously, the most favorable forecast for Team Canada came from Soviet coach Vsevolod Bobrov. He predicted that the best Canadian play was yet to come.

"Team Canada has not yet been on form," he said. "They had not trained much and were overconfident. Now they will be stronger. They will take these games more seriously. And they will be in better condition."

They were kind words, but the NHL embarrassment had not yet ended. In the pre-game ceremonies before the fifth contest Phil Esposito skated toward center ice to accept a bouquet of flowers. Suddenly the magnificent Bruin skater wound up on his backside. "One of the flower stems had fallen off," Esposito later explained. "I stepped on it and was on my behind in a flash!"

That proved to be only the start of Team Canada's troubles. Twice the NHL aces built a three-goal lead, but the Russians struck back to tie the score. Ultimately the home team went ahead to capture the match, 5–4. "The Russians never let up," said coach Sinden. "They just keep coming at you."

The Soviets had now won three games, tied one and lost one. Another victory would clinch the series. With three more games left on friendly Moscow ice, they seemed sure of triumph.

Nothing suggested that Team Canada was capable of a comeback. Apart from the three losses, the Canadian spirit had been further weakened by the walkout of several players. New York Ranger captain Vic Hadfield returned home to Canada because he disagreed with Sinden's coaching policies.

"Take a look at the captain of the Rangers going home because he can't win a place on the team," said

II

As the teams are being presented to Moscow hockey fans, Team Canada star Phil Esposito takes an undignified fall.

John Forristall, one of Team Canada's trainers. His biting tone illustrated the ill-will on the Canada squad.

Team Canada may have been down, but something clicked in the sixth game. Neither team scored in the first period, and before the second period was two minutes old, the Russians had gone ahead on Yuri Liapkin's goal against goalie Ken Dryden. It was the eighth time the Russians had beaten the Montreal goalie by shooting low to his left, an obvious aspect of their strategy.

But then Team Canada returned to the offense. Rod Gilbert intercepted a Russian pass and skimmed the puck to teammate Dennis Hull. Hull fired at Tretiak and the Soviet goalie made the first save but allowed the rubber to rebound back to Hull. Dennis' second shot was true, and although nobody realized it at the time, that was the turning point in the entire series!

Less than a minute and a half later Yvan Cournoyer converted Red Berenson's pass into another Team Canada goal. Then came a third score, this one from the stick of Toronto's Paul Henderson. The Russians struck back once to pull within one goal, but Dryden repulsed them throughout the third period, and Team Canada emerged with a heartening 3–2 triumph.

Two games remained for Team Canada and two wins were needed. It seemed impossible as the seventh game unfolded. The Russians mounted a 2–1 lead in the first period. But late in the period Phil Esposito displayed his unique leadership qualities and tied the game with a goal.

Goalie Tony Esposito looks stunned as Russia's Yevgeny Mishakov flies into the net during the sixth game.

Neither team scored in a tense middle frame, and then the clubs traded goals early in the third period. Now it was 3–3 and the stage was set for high drama. If the Russians could hold off the visitors and come up with a tie, they would come out winners of the series. If Team Canada could go ahead to stay, they would have a chance to win the eighth game and the series.

As the clock approached the 18th minute of the last period, Serge Savard of Team Canada passed the puck to Paul Henderson, who confronted a pair of Russian defensemen, a seemingly impregnable barrier. What followed was one of the most dramatic scores in the entire series.

"I tried to push the puck through the legs of one of them," said Henderson, "and I got a bit of a break on it. The puck hit his skate, deflecting it to his right, and that gave me the chance I needed. While he was looking for it, I moved around him. I had pretty good balance when I let the shot go. What I mean is, I put the puck exactly where I wanted it to go. Upstairs."

Henderson was knocked down on the play, but he kept his eyes riveted on the net. His frown turned to a gigantic smile as he watched the net bulge. At 17:54 of the final period Team Canada had gone ahead to stay. Final score: 4–3. Henderson had managed to tie the series, each team having won three and tied one. Everything now hinged on the outcome of the eighth and final match.

According to some observers, the normally methodical Russians were now in a panic. One loss at home would have been bad enough, but two straight defeats was humiliating. Now they faced the prospects of three losses in a row and defeat in the series. Despite their great performance so far, it was clear the final game meant as much to the Soviets as it did to Team Canada.

After two periods of hectic play it looked as if the Russians would prevail. Their splendid pattern passing plays and vigorous skating enabled them to mount a 5–3 lead in front of Tretiak's heroic goaltending. Team Canada gave no promise of reviving in the third period, and Ken Dryden seemed shaky in the nets.

But the prideful members of Team Canada believed otherwise. "We're better hockey players," insisted Peter Mahovlich. Then the NHL skaters went out in the third period to prove just how right he was. Phil Esposito scored at 2:27 to pull Team Canada within one goal. Nearly 11 minutes later Yvan Cournoyer tied the score.

Now the Soviets are hanging on for dear life, hoping to escape with a tie. But Team Canada lunges for the Russian jugular, shooting for a sixth goal.

With less than a minute to go, the Canadians have made several great attempts, but the game still is tied, 5–5. Coach Sinden calls Peter Mahovlich to the bench and orders Paul Henderson onto the ice in his place. Phil Esposito gets the puck in front of the Russian goal and shoots. Tretiak makes the save but allows the puck to trickle away.

Henderson is there and shoots again. Tretiak stops it again but cannot control the puck. Henderson fires again and this time the puck slides under Tretiak's pads and into the goal!

That's all there was to it. Seconds later Team Canada skated off the ice with a 6–5 triumph and a

With seconds to go, Paul Henderson fires the puck past Tretiak to win the eighth and decisive game.

series victory—four games won, three games lost and one tied.

Coach Sinden called it the greatest hockey game ever played and others seconded his motion. Certainly it was one of the most exciting.

But when the excitement died down, observers

The Canadian fans, in Moscow to cheer their team on, are delighted by Team Canada's amazing comeback victory.

agreed that the Soviets had proven themselves equal to the best professionals in North America. "I don't think any of those Russians would have trouble finding jobs in the NHL," said Peter Mahovlich. "But only three or four of them would be invited to the All-Star Game."

The Team Canada–Russian series had reverberations which will be heard for years to come. It set big-league and amateur coaches to examining the Soviet style of play and conditioning techniques. The excitement created by the series brought new popularity for hockey particularly in Europe, and a European Professional League was organized with the backing of Detroit Red Wings owner Bruce Norris.

Some experts argued that the Canadians were the real losers because they had been favored to win eight straight games and were fortunate to squeeze out a last-minute triumph in the final game.

Perhaps the most accurate apraisal of all was made by Canadian author Henk W. Hoppener, who wrote when it was over: "We won the games. We lost a legend."

12
SHER-WOOD
SHER-WOOD
SHER-WOOD

Index

Page numbers in italics refer to photographs.